SIMONE DE BEAUVOIR

MODERN LITERATURE MONOGRAPHS

GENERAL EDITOR: *Lina Mainiero*

SIMONE DE BEAUVOIR

Robert D. Cottrell

Frederick Ungar Publishing Co.
New York

For my parents

Second Printing, 1976

Copyright © 1975 by Frederick Ungar Publishing Co., Inc.
Printed in the United States of America
Library of Congress Catalog Card Number: 74-34131
Designed by Anita Duncan
ISBN: 0-8044-2132-3

Contents

Chronology

1908: Born January 9 in Paris.

1913: Starts formal schooling in October at Cours Désir.

1917: Meets Elizabeth (Zaza) Mabille in October.

1919: Family suffers a loss of income and moves into a less expensive apartment.

1925: Studies literature with Robert Garric at Saint Mary's Institute in suburban Neuilly and mathematics at the Catholic Institute in Paris.

1926: Joins Garric's "Social Teams" (*Équipes sociales*) and for a brief time teaches literature at a center for working girls. Studies philosophy at the Sorbonne.

1929: Meets Sartre. Zaza dies. Receives her *agrégation de philosophie*. Teaches Latin at Lycée Victor Duruy in Paris.

1931: Teaches philosophy in a lycée in Marseilles.

1932: Teaches philosophy in a lycée in Rouen where she stays for four years.

1936: Teaches philosophy in a lycée in Paris for next seven years.

1938: Begins writing *L'Invitée* in October.

1943: *L'Invitée*. Quits teaching.

1944: *Pyrrhus et Cinéas*.

1945: Lectures in Portugal in February. *Les Bouches inutiles.*

1946: *Tous les hommes sont mortels.*

1947:   *Pour une morale de l'ambiguïté.* Visits the United
        States for the first time. Meets Nelson Algren in
        Chicago.

1948:   *L'Amérique au jour le jour. L'Existentialisme et la
        sagesse des nations.* Spends two months in the
        United States, mostly with Algren. Travels to Cen-
        tral America with Algren.

1949:   *Le Deuxième Sexe.*

1950:   Spends two months in the United States, mostly
        at Algren's cottage on Lake Michigan. Travels with
        Sartre to Africa and throughout Europe. End of
        liaison with Algren.

1952:   In December begins liaison with Claude Lanzmann.

1954:   *Les Mandarins.* Awarded Prix Goncourt. For next
        several years, involved in various movements sup-
        porting Algerian independence and North Vietnam.

1955:   *Privilèges.* Visits China. From now on, she and
        Sartre spend most of their summers in Rome.

1957:   *La Longue Marche.*

1958:   *Mémoires d'une jeune fille rangée.* End of liaison
        with Lanzmann.

1960:   *Brigitte Bardot and the Lolita Syndrome. La Force
        de l'âge.*

1962:   *Djamila Boupacha,* in collaboration with Gisèle
        Halimi. Visits the Soviet Union.

1963:   *La Force des choses.* Mother dies.

1964:   *Une Mort très douce.*

1966:   *Les Belles Images.*

1967:   Participates in Russell Tribunal in Copenhagen.
        La Femme rompue.

1970:   *La Vieillesse.*

1972:   *Tout compte fait.*

The Dutiful
Daughter

Ever since childhood Simone de Beauvoir has had an acute sense of her particular, unique destiny and of her mission to recount that destiny. Earnest and relentlessly energetic, she has always wished to be a useful, indeed, even an indispensable member of the human community. With a taste for self-denial and Spartan living that Anglo-Saxons might characterize as puritan, she has long been a dissenter. However, it would be a mistake to exaggerate her rebelliousness. Her rejection of certain of the values and conventions of the rather rigid French bourgeois society in which she was brought up was accompanied by an affirmation of the competitive spirit—the compelling urge to make one's own way and to succeed—that lies at the heart of the bourgeois mentality. A one-time professor of philosophy but not a philosopher in the strict sense of the word, she is descended, by temperament and cast of mind, from those eighteenth-century intellectual gadflies known as *philosophes*. With them she shares an implacable drive to happiness, an optimism, a thirst for justice, and a faith in the rightness of her role as the conscience of a generation.

Numerous times throughout her voluminous work Beauvoir asserts that one of the goals she has pursued most obstinately (the word is hers) has been to strip away the hypocrisies, prejudices, lies, and mystifications that obstruct our perception of reality and prevent us from seeing the truth. Ever since her earliest years when, at the age of four or five, she enjoyed imparting her superior knowledge of the world to her younger sister, she has had a strong urge to teach. One of the profound impulses of her work has always been to combat ignorance or indifference and to provoke change. Convinced that a great man is one who contributes to the intellectual and moral elevation of humanity as a whole, the teenaged Simone—with the idealism, seriousness of purpose, and missionary zeal that are so attractive in the young girl but at times so exasperating in the adult woman—formulated a credo from which she never really deviated: "perfect myself, enrich myself, and express myself in a work that will help others to live."[1]

An even more basic impulse in her work is an irresistible urge to communicate her own experience, to re-create her own life. Aware of the fact that she does not possess the kind of inventive imagination that characterizes the very greatest creators of fiction, Beauvoir, who nevertheless has written several important novels, maintains that the creation of a fictional world has never been her intention. In 1972 at the age of sixty-four she looked back on the many books she had written and declared that her mission as a writer was not to create an *oeuvre d'art*, but rather to communicate as directly as possible the feel of her own life.

Indeed, Beauvoir's novels, essays, sociological studies, and travel books all reflect the tenor of the author's life at the time they were written. However, they present a fragmentary picture; they do not succeed in conveying the sense of coherence and inner necessity which Beauvoir experiences in her own life and which she would like to communicate to the reader. Thus it was perhaps inevitable that she should eventually turn to autobiography. Contrary to a number of fashionable literary critics in the middle of the twentieth century, she has repeatedly affirmed that a book takes on its true meaning only if one knows the circumstances surrounding its inception and the point of view or personality of the author.[2] In an effort to explain who she is and to situate the context in which each of her books was written, Beauvoir composed from 1958 to 1972 the four massive volumes that con-

stitute her autobiography—the work which, among all
her works, she especially likes and which figures among
her most widely read works both in France and
abroad.

Writing an autobiography is a delicate under-
taking. The nineteenth-century historian Renan
warned readers of his own *Souvenirs* that what one
says about oneself is always poetry. There is no doubt
that in re-creating her childhood and early adulthood
Beauvoir structured her early experience in light of
her later beliefs. As the high priestess of atheistic
existentialism and the most ardent disciple of Jean-
Paul Sartre, she recounts her early years in such a
way that the story of her youth is an illustration of
certain key tenets of existentialist doctrine. Chief
among these is the belief that man is free and that to
live authentically he must assume his freedom by performing a vigorous act which, in the vocabulary of
existentialism, is usually called a "project." When
Beauvoir writes that man is transcendence, she simply
means that by a continuous series of "projects" man
repeatedly reaffirms his autonomy and fashions his
own life. Furthermore, "what one transcends," declares
Beauvoir, "is always one's past. One's future envelops
one's past and cannot be built without it."[3]

In Beauvoir's scheme of things, the future is
usually built by reacting *against* the past. Her notion
of "project" generally contains a sense of refusal or
rejection. Transcendence implies a progression from
relative inauthenticity to greater authenticity, from
the passive state of an object or thing that is complete
in itself to the active state of a subject or agent that
is incomplete because its future is undetermined. Contrary to an object, a subject constructs its own future
by its choices and acts. Passivity is the being of things,
whereas choice is that of human beings. In Sartre's
famous terminology, which is often used by Beauvoir,

the former category of being is called *être-en-soi* or being-in-itself, the latter, *être-pour-soi* or being-for-itself. To the extent that human beings refuse to assume their freedom and falsify their existence by accepting pre-existing roles that relieve them of the often painful necessity of choice, they live in the mode of."being-in-itself" rather than "being-for-itself." That is to say, they live a life that is not authentically human, for, to use another Sartrean pair of words repeated countless numbers of times by Beauvoir, their lives are characterized by "immanence" rather than "transcendence."

In *Mémoires d'une jeune fille rangée* (*Memoirs of a Dutiful Daughter*)—the first and most famous volume of her autobiography—Beauvoir, with the ironic tone of someone who is convinced that he has left behind all idolatry and pettifoggery, reconstructs the first twenty-one years of her life. Her family (parents, grandparents, aunts, uncles, cousins) represents the world of immanence that the young Simone strove to transcend. An absorbingly interesting book, *Mémoires d'une jeune fille rangée* is essentially the story of the author's transcendence, consistently presented as an exemplary rejection of the bourgeois values that dominated her parents' world.

The family into which Simone de Beauvoir was born on January 9, 1908 was, as she describes it, a typical upper-middle-class Parisian family. Her father, a lawyer, was gregarious, passionately fond of the theater, elegant and charming in a rather brittle way, ultranationalistic, and totally indifferent to matters of religion. Her mother, who had been educated in a provincial convent before moving to Paris at the time of her marriage, accepted the rigid moral conventions of the Catholic bourgeoisie as the embodiment of human and divine wisdom.

Beauvoir's childhood was happy. In her mature years the author, who often spoke of her incurable optimism, declared that no one has a greater aptitude for happiness than she, adding that she sees a direct relationship between a happy childhood and the capacity for joy later in life. Healthy, bursting with vitality, she began auspiciously what she later called her fundamental enterprise in life: appropriating the world for herself.

From the very first pages of *Mémoires d'une jeune fille rangée* it becomes clear that Beauvoir wishes to stress certain of her character traits. Two and a half years older than her sister Hélène (called Poupette), she was, as far back as she can remember, proud of being the first child. Much as any intelligent, lively, and self-confident child might do, young Simone began exploring the world around her.

What is not so usual, however, is the manner in which the adult author describes the child's curiosity and appetite for life. She begins by saying: "Wholeheartedly I took advantage of the privilege of children for whom beauty, luxury, and happiness are things that can be eaten."[4] The world is a table covered with exquisite comestibles—candied fruits and sweets —which the child, with a shiver of sensuous delight, seizes and devours. After a lengthy paragraph in which objects are presented as if they existed solely for the gastronomical pleasure of young Simone, the author remarks curiously that even much later in life she tended to view the world as a morsel that she would like to pop into her mouth and crack between her teeth. Walking through the countryside, the mature Beauvoir felt the urge to bite into flowering almond trees. And in New York, she longed to taste the neon lights, which seemed like giant sweetmeats.

Perhaps we need not go so far as the Dominican

priest A.-M. Henry, who saw in Beauvoir's adult attitudes—especially in her persistent hunger and enduring thirst for experience, her gluttony as she herself puts it—a prolongation of the egocentrism that marks the oral stage of a child's development.[5] Nevertheless, it is plain that in this long and remarkable paragraph, placed as it is at the beginning of the *Mémoires*, Beauvoir intends to suggest the nature of her relationship with the world. Her choice of words is revelatory: covet, explore, conquer, and especially possess, which is repeated in a rapturous litany.

Pride in being first and eagerness to possess as much of experience as possible are traits that the author immediately discerns in the youthful Simone. No doubt they remain in some form or other in the mature woman. But in the context of *Mémoires d'une jeune fille rangée* they are something more than personal character traits. They are also a reflection of the bourgeois society in which Beauvoir was reared. Here we approach one of the fundamental features of Beauvoir's portrayal of her childhood and adolescence. A child, because of his passivity (Beauvoir uses the phrase "the passivity of childhood"[6]), lives primarily in the world of immanence. He does not make his own values; he is not autonomous. He embraces the values of those around him and fits himself into pre-existing roles that others have created for him. When Beauvoir writes that a child lives in a metaphysically privileged state, she means that his world is regulated by unwritten laws that, for him, seem natural and indisputable. Not yet realizing his freedom, he does not yet understand that things have no meaning in themselves and that it is up to him to create their meaning. He does not yet comprehend that the future, too, is meaningless, utterly empty, and can be filled only by his own choices. In short, he feels secure because to him things seem "necessary" when in fact they are "contingent" (two words that figure prominently in existentialist vocabulary).

This is, of course, a perfectly valid philosophical position. What is less valid, however, is the cunning manner in which Beauvoir covertly equates the meta-physically privileged state of childhood with the economically privileged state of the bourgeoisie. The two are not commensurate, and if they are artfully equated (an unacceptable procedure, I believe, because it blurs crucial distinctions), it is for ideological purposes. Ostensibly speaking about the child's privilege of perceiving beauty, luxury, and happiness in terms of things that are edible, Beauvoir is in fact describing not only herself as a child but the privileged milieu in which she lived—a milieu she later came to hate.

Thus young Simone's pride and possessiveness, both of which might seem to be perfectly normal in a psychological context, become an ironic comment on the bourgeoisie whose characteristics—in this case, arrogance and greedy materialism—the child reflects. When Beauvoir describes herself as having been in-sufferably smug and complacent, as having reveled in her "glorious singularity,"[7] she is not confessing. Her strategy is to damn the bourgeoisie by ridiculing the young bourgeois girl she once was. Irony informs nearly every page of *Mémoires d'une jeune fille rangée.*

An almost inevitable consequence of this ideo-logical impulse is a tendency to present people in caricatural terms. Her father's passion for the theater and his talent for acting are reduced to a "fondness for appearances,"[8] suggesting an inability or an un-willingness to face reality squarely. He becomes slightly ridiculous and vaguely contemptible. The spectacle of a famous writer describing her parents as if they were stock characters in a trifling comedy is at times disconcerting. Indeed, nearly all the adults in *Mé-*

moires d'une jeune fille rangé have a clownish or inauthentic quality about them. Beauvoir's prejudice is such that a bourgeois—unless he is in a position of political power, in which case he becomes a monstrous incarnation of evil—is essentially a shallow, comic figure.

No character in *Mémoires d'une jeune fille rangée* is presented more ironically than young Simone herself. Her world was dominated by a kind of dualism. Mankind was divided hierarchically into two antithetical classes; on top reigned her family while "in the lower depths crouched the rest of the human race."[9] "My universe," notes Beauvoir early in her memoirs, "was divided into two major categories—Good and Evil. I inhabited the region of the Good."[10]

Her faith in the existence of these two categories and her assurance that her rightful place was in the former were constantly reaffirmed by her religious instruction:

A whole race of supernatural beings hovered over me solicitously. As soon as I learned to walk, Mama took me to church. She showed me, in wax, in plaster, and painted on the walls, portraits of little Jesus, of God, of the Virgin, and of angels, one of whom, like our maid Louise, was assigned exclusively to my service. My heaven was studded with a myriad of benevolent eyes.[11]

The fact that her father did not share her mother's religious convictions—convictions which Beauvoir, writing from her later atheistic point of view, presents as superficial and conventional—did not disturb her own faith. It did, however, compel young Simone to separate her intellectual life (incarnated in her father who lauded her scholastic achievements) from her spiritual life (which was directed by her mother). She was convinced that sanctity and intelligence belonged to two quite different spheres. In a revealing sentence she remarks: "Thus I set God apart from life and the world, and this attitude was to have a profound influence on my later development."[12]

Indeed, as she grew older, she gradually ceased to believe first in the infallibility of her father, then in the existence of God. Both in her *Mémoires* and in a long and important interview with critic Francis Jeanson, Beauvoir attached considerable importance to the fact that during puberty, when her face was pimply, her whole demeanor charmless, she felt abandoned by her father who not only lost interest in her but displayed a marked preference for her younger sister. Her father's betrayal (as she interprets the situation) signaled her gradual loss of faith in the principles that heretofore structured her world. In her re-creation of her youth, Beauvoir uses her fall from paternal grace to presage her falling out with God.

Her God, she explained, had existed outside the world. As the adolescent Simone became more and more interested in things around her, she eventually came to feel that her passionate interest in the world was incompatible with faith in this supranatural deity. Because of her extremism, as she puts it, she was convinced that she must choose between God and the world. She chose the world. Unwilling to renounce "earthly pleasures,"[13] she renounced God, and discovered to her amazement that she had not believed in Him for some time.

Her adolescence was marked not only by her loss of belief in God and by what was, after all, a rather normal reaction to parental authority. It was also marked by the discovery of her own mortality. "One afternoon in Paris I realized that I was condemned to die. I was alone in the apartment, and I made no attempt to repress my despair. I screamed, and tore at the red carpet."[14] In *Mémoires d'une jeune fille rangée*, Beauvoir recounts this incident immediately after having discussed her loss of faith, thus suggesting a causal relationship in her mind between God's absence and her own eventual absence from the world. One could of course argue that this causal relationship is spurious because perception of God's absence or presence and perception of one's mortality are of a different order. What is important, however, is that her sudden awareness of mortality seemed to her to confirm God's absence. Indeed, with the disappearance of God, the principle of necessity seemed to vanish from the world, leaving in its place the troubling concepts of contingency and mortality.

Awareness of death can be, and often is, a disturbing experience for a child. Still, I suspect that few children react with the violent rage of young Simone. Indeed, throughout her *Mémoires* she emphasizes her childish rages, which for the most part are not directed, as here, against the human condition, but against the necessity of being a child in an adult world. She sees in her tantrums, in her outbursts of revolt, an intimation of her later philosophical and political positions, which will be characterized by dissent.

Just as the charged vocabulary she uses when talking about the metaphysically privileged state of childhood betrays an intent to comment on the economically privileged state of the bourgeoisie, so the existentialist vocabulary she often uses when mentioning her childish rages reveals her tendency to describe events and circumstances in her childhood in such a way that they substantiate certain tenets of existentialism. Referring to her childhood fits of anger, for example, she remarks that grown-ups continually thwarted her will and that she felt as if she were the prey of the consciousness of adults. Her youthful rages are thus interpreted in light of two Hegelian notions that would later become important ingredients in existentialism—the master-slave dialectics, which Sartre would popularize in France in the 1940s, and the related idea, re-interpreted and given greater emotional force by Husserl, that each consciousness, in its struggle to remain autonomous, continually opposes the attempt of every other consciousness to subjugate it.

Despite occasional metaphysical insights, as Beauvoir ironically calls her youthful intuitions into the nature of things, young Simone certainly did not spend her time brooding over contingency, mortality, and the like. The most diligent of schoolgirls, she was much too busy staying at the top of her class for that. In her *Mémoires*, she portrays herself as one of those bright, competitive little schoolgirls who always know the right answers. This portrait, however, is softened by three important elements in her character: her capacity for friendship, her affection for her cousin Jacques, and her love of nature.

When she was nine years old, Beauvoir met Elizabeth Mabille (called Zaza) who was the same age and attended the same Catholic school. (The school bore the enticing name, Désir, after its founder.) Zaza's exuberance and spontaneousness immediately dazzled the more conventional Simone. The two girls soon became fast friends, although as Beauvoir notes, Zaza was much more important to her than she to Zaza. For the next twelve years her admiration and friendship for Zaza would be one of the most significant factors in her life. It permitted her to break out of the increasingly stifling confines of the family. Equally important, her affection for Zaza took her out of herself. If she sometimes still considered herself exceptional, she never again, so she says, considered herself unique.

Although the two girls shared many common interests, including a passion for literature, it is the difference in their situations and destinies that Beauvoir stresses. Whereas Beauvoir eventually rejected the Catholic bourgeois society of her parents, Zaza, because of a deep-rooted sense of insecurity as well as unwavering devotion to her mother (who is portrayed as totally unworthy of her daughter's affection), never lost her religious faith nor rejected the role of dutiful daughter. With considerable tenderness and understanding, Beauvoir analyzes the reasons—psychological as well as social—that prevented Zaza from gaining the freedom and authenticity for which both girls so desperately struggled. When Zaza eventually fell in love with a young man of whom her mother disapproved, she was unable to free herself from her family and follow the dictates of her heart. Physically exhausted and emotionally torn between two conflicting demands, she died, perhaps of meningitis, in 1929 at the age of twenty-one. "Together we had fought against the murky fate that awaited us," notes Beauvoir in the last sentence of *Mémoires d'une jeune fille rangée*, "and for a long time I believed that I had paid for my freedom with her death."[15]

Indeed, Zaza's death haunted Beauvoir's imagination for years. Her first earnest efforts at writing a work that would launch her literary career were fictionalized accounts of Zaza's death. Generally unsuccessful, they were not published, and it was not until she wrote her memoirs that she managed to erect a splendid monument to Zaza's memory. Beauvoir held the bourgeoisie responsible for Zaza's death. Although Beauvoir was well on her way to freedom from Church and family before Zaza's death, it is likely that her friend's spiritual torment and death partly explain the intensity of her condemnation of the bourgeois milieu.

As she approached the age of twenty, Beauvoir was attracted to her cousin Jacques Laiguillon. Her rather vague and indecisive love for Jacques, who was six months her senior, contributed, as did her friendship for Zaza, to the expansion of her sensibility. Furthermore, Jacques, who was soon to pass out of her life without leaving any regrets behind, introduced her to contemporary literature, which she would no doubt have discovered on her own, but not until sometime later. Jacques also introduced her to "the poetry of bars."[16] Occasionally alone, more often with Jacques or with her sister, Beauvoir for a time frequented the little bars that dotted the Parisian scene in the 1920s. Coming from a straitlaced milieu and basically rather prudish herself, she discovered with a shiver of delight and an exhilarating sense of freedom the world of jazz, dry martinis, and gin fizzes. Typically, she restricted herself to one martini or, at the most, two gin fizzes. "The attraction that bars and dance halls had for me," she remarks lucidly, "was derived in large part from their illicit character."[17]

From her earliest childhood, Beauvoir had spent her summers in the country, usually at her paternal uncle's estate in central France. Contrasting with her bookish life in Paris, her life in the country was an endless series of explorations of the natural world. A vigorous love of nature, at times almost Rousseauistic in its intensity, is an essential element in Beauvoir's character.

God's discreet departure did not mean that Beauvoir discarded the moral code for which He had been the guarantor. She simply secularized notions such as duty and merit which, all her life, would continue to figure prominently in her austere code of ethics. Indeed, one of the principles that order Beauvoir's world is a secularized and politicized form of the Christian dichotomy of good and evil—the polarization of mankind into the saved and the damned.

Furthermore, the mature author constantly fluctuates between two opposing positions, both of which may well have their roots in her religious education: at times she tends to see herself as representative of humanity, a kind of prefiguration of what mankind will become once it has shaken off the shackles of inauthenticity; more frequently she seems to speak in the name of the elect (mostly Marxist intellectuals) who are irrevocably separated from the mass of the damned (mostly bourgeois dullards).

Nor did God's disappearance diminish Beauvoir's "thirst for necessity"[18]—one of the traits most firmly ingrained in her character and one of the themes most persistently woven into the fabric of her work. No longer dependent on God, she soon realized that she herself would have to provide the necessity which would give her life coherence and meaning. Once again the order in which Beauvoir relates events and situations is highly significant. In the pages that immediately follow her account of God's effacement, she dwells on the extreme importance of books in her youth. Two fictional heroines particularly impressed her. First, she recognized herself in Jo, one of the sisters in Louise May Alcott's *Little Women*. Somewhat later she read George Eliot's *The Mill on the Floss*, which had an even more profound effect upon her. Although she saw herself in Maggie Tulliver, she identified, not with the fictional character, but with author George Eliot. "One day," she promised herself, "an adolescent, another me, will bathe with tears a novel in which I shall tell my own story."[19]

She had in fact been writing since she was eight years old. However, after her loss of faith she turned to literature with a definite sense of vocation; literature would assure her of an immortality that would compensate for the eternity she had lost. There was no longer a God to love her, but she would burn in millions of hearts. Her life, she thought, would be a lovely story come true—a story she would make up as she went along. At the age of fifteen she answered the question "What do you want to be?" in a friend's keepsake book with the words: "A famous writer." "I coveted that future," she adds, "to the exclusion of any other."[20]

In addition to dreaming of becoming a famous writer, she dreamt, as girls do, of falling in love. "In this area, as in all others," she notes, "I had a thirst for necessity. I would have to feel as if the chosen one were predestined for me. I would fall in love the day that a man would subjugate me by his intelligence, his knowledge, his authority."[21] Clearly, her cousin Jacques could not pass muster. Given Beauvoir's intelligence, knowledge, and authority it might seem as if the odds were against such a man appearing. That he did appear though, in the personage of Jean-Paul Sartre, was, as Beauvoir acknowledges, a piece of good luck for which she was ever grateful.

She met Sartre, who was three years her senior, in 1929. Both were preparing for the *agrégation de philosophie*, the most prestigious academic degree offered in France. The previous year Sartre had failed his examination because he had neglected to prepare adequately the section dealing with the history of philosophy. Beauvoir was eager to take her examination as soon as possible and threw herself into her studies with the diligence and energy so typical of her.

Ever since 1925, when she had completed her secondary education at the Cours Désir, she had been studying in various educational institutions, preparing for an academic career. Fearful of the effects that the reputed immorality of students at the Sorbonne might have on their daughter, her parents first sent her in 1926 to the Catholic Institute where she studied mathematics and to Saint Mary's Institute in Neuilly, a suburb of Paris, where she studied literature.

One of her professors at Neuilly was Robert Garric, a fervent Catholic who, in addition to his professorial duties, had founded a social service organization to work with the poor. In her memoirs, Beauvoir couches her boundless admiration for Garric in terms that make of his ethical stance a prefiguration of existentialist ethics: "At last I met a man who, instead of submitting to destiny, had chosen his life. His existence—endowed with a goal, with a meaning —incarnated an idea and was governed by an overriding necessity."[22] Seeing in Garric the example of a life devoted to a useful cause, his admiring pupil promised herself that her life, too, would be a life of service.

Despite a certain amount of parental displeasure, Beauvoir enrolled in the Sorbonne in 1927, studying Greek, philology, and especially philosophy. Then in 1929 she took the competitive state examination for the *agrégation*. The examiners were impressed and ranked her second. At the top of the list was her friend of the past few months, Jean-Paul Sartre.

It did not take Beauvoir long to discern the difference between Sartre and her cousin Jacques. "It was the first time in my life I felt that I was intellectually dominated by someone."[23] Summing up her feelings toward Sartre, she writes: "Sartre corresponded exactly to the wish I made when I was fifteen years old. He was the double in whom I found all my manias raised to the level of incandescence. With him I would always be able to share everything. When I left him at the beginning of August, I knew that he would always be a part of my life."[24]

With the disappearance of Zaza and the appearance of Sartre in the same year, *Mémoires d'une jeune fille rangé* comes to a close. Poised on the threshold of her career as a professor of philosophy and certain that she had found in Sartre a man whom she could love, Beauvoir was ready to abandon the role of daughter, more or less dutiful, that she had played for some twenty years, and to embark on the arduous but exhilarating task of fashioning her own future. The prime of life, she felt, was just around the corner.

2

Transcending

the Past

The second volume of Beauvoir's autobiography (*La Force de l'âge* or *The Prime of Life*) covers the years 1929-1944. There are two basic components in the book: the smaller consists of brief accounts of the momentous events that were taking place in Europe during the 1930s; the larger by far is the author's portrayal of her own life, which she presents as a strictly individual pursuit, totally isolated from politics. Up until 1939 the two strands are separate. Political events are presented in a few compact pages that are isolated from the rest of the text; often they are placed at the beginning of the various chapters.

This structural pattern corresponds to one of Beauvoir's fundamental intents in this volume; writing in the postwar years, when she had adopted the existentialist notion of commitment and had drawn closer to theoretical Marxism, she condemns, sometimes directly, more often by ironic comment, the apolitical life she and Sartre led during the 1930s. When war broke out in 1939, Beauvoir (Sartre less so) was caught completely unawares. She who had thought of herself as "pure consciousness and pure will"[1] was, like millions of other Europeans, swept up in the currents of history. "I now came to know," she writes in the pompously rhetorical style that mars more than a few pages of the autobiography, "that in the very marrow of my being I was bound up with my contemporaries. I discovered that this dependence had another side to it: my responsibility."[2]

The year 1939 marks, then, a crucial turning point in Beauvoir's life. The separation between herself and the world is obliterated and she falls into history. In the pages devoted to the years 1940-44, the account of her personal life and that of external events no longer form two strands that run parallel to each other without touching. They are now woven into a single narrative movement.

In 1929 Beauvoir had thought that she had shed the notions and prejudices of the society in which she had been brought up. Indeed, she did reject certain of the forms and traditional rites valued by her society. She and Sartre, for example, decided not to marry. Resorting to existentialist jargon, she quotes Sartre as explaining that theirs was a "necessary love"[3] which was indestructible; they should therefore not deprive themselves of occasional "contingent loves" that might prove to be enriching and rewarding experiences. Furthermore, they intended to pursue their respective academic careers and so anticipated long periods of separation. Neither of them wanted children. Sartre therefore suggested in 1929 that, instead of getting married, they sign a conjugal pact, subject to cancellation or renegotiation after two years.

By 1931, however, there was no need for them to make another pact. They were sure of their feelings for each other. When in the spring of that year Sartre was offered a position as professor of philosophy in a lycée in Le Havre and Beauvoir a similar position at the opposite end of the country in Marseilles, he suggested that they get married. However, afraid of alienating each other by changing a freely chosen relationship into an irrevocable bond, they rejected the idea once and for all.

It was with a sense of exhilaration that Beauvoir arrived in Marseilles in the fall of 1931 to begin her teaching duties. Coming out of the train station, she paused for a moment at the top of the flight of stairs descending to the city and, like Balzac's ambitious hero Rastignac who, viewing Paris from a hill, vowed to conquer it, Beauvoir surveyed the world she was soon to make her own. She stopped at the first "Room for rent" sign she saw. The room happened to be above a bustling cafe, and was equipped with a divan, a few bookshelves and a solid table at which she could write. She rented it immediately and rushed out to explore Marseilles.

There is something decidedly appealing in Beauvoir's indifference to luxury. All her life she would avoid fashionable restaurants and smart hotels. In many respects a puritan, she welcomed difficulty and prized effort. An indefatigable hiker, she often strapped a knapsack on her back and spent hours tramping around the beautiful countryside near Marseilles. For the next ten years or more she and Sartre would spend every summer exploring France or visiting Spain, Italy, or Greece. Often they hiked, Beauvoir marching on ahead, Sartre following, somewhat breathless but usually in the best of spirits.

After one year in Marseilles she was transferred to Rouen, close to Le Havre where Sartre was still teaching, and also to Paris. Then in 1936 both she and Sartre were assigned to Paris where they were teaching when the war broke out.

The prewar years were active ones for Beauvoir. In addition to her teaching, she read voraciously, discovering Hemingway, Faulkner, Dos Passos, Heidegger, and Husserl among others. She frequented cafes, theatres, cinemas, art galleries, and spent hours talking with friends, especially Sartre. Perhaps more than any of her other books, *La Force de l'âge* expresses what she calls "the joy of living" ("la gaïté d'exister").[4] No doubt critic René Girard is right when he asserts that Beauvoir occasionally succumbs to the old myth of romantic spontaneity.[5] She tends to react to things, places, people, and ideas with either extravagent enthusiasm or peremptory disdain. She moves from one exuberant revelation to another, and, like Annie in Sartre's *La Nausée* or *Nausea*, 1938, (with whom she has more than one trait in common) she exults in "perfect moments"[6] of spontaneous insight.

There is in Beauvoir's breathless enthusiasm a certain studied resolve to remain young. Indeed, she recognized that both she and Sartre made a cult of youth and valued highly its tumultuousness, its revolts, its freedom, and its intransigence. Adulthood inspired only disgust in them. In fact, Beauvoir believed that the severe depression from which Sartre suffered for almost a year in the mid-thirties—a depression marked by recurring visions of crabs and lobsters—was caused in part by his refusal to accept the responsibilities and conventions of adulthood.

Beauvoir's impatient rejection of adult mores has, like her admiration for a sometimes hazy spontaneity, many elements in common with the rebelliousness so dear to the romantics of the nineteenth century. Even the revolutionary politics she and Sartre adopted later has many a feature of romantic revolt. Commenting on their antibourgeois stance during the thirties, she declares: "We hated Sunday crowds, proper ladies and gentlemen, the provinces, family life, children, and all varieties of humanism."[7]

Despite the intemperate combativeness of her language, Beauvoir here expresses something more than the naïve desire to ape youthful rebelliousness. She is also stating, albeit rather crudely in this passage, a notion that is fundamental to much of her (and Sartre's) work: namely, rejection of the bourgeoisie's worship of the past, and condemnation of a humanism that has become limited to a particular social class and to a few countries in western Europe. After the war, this rejection would be expressed in terms of left-wing ideology (mainly the notion of class struggle) and political activism. Looking back on their attitudes during the thirties, Beauvoir condemns the purely verbal form that their "antibourgeois anarchism"[8] assumed during those years. Entrenched in the back of a somber bar, Beauvoir and Sartre spent hours

castigating the bourgeoisie, weaving around themselves a silky cocoon of words that protected them
from the "real world." Their morality, she says disapprovingly, remained idealistic and bourgeois. They
mistakenly imagined that they were representative of
humanity as a whole. In their egotism and arrogance
they unwittingly demonstrated their identity with the
very privileged class they thought they were repudi-
ating.[9]

Although the animated bustle of life is no doubt
the dominant strain in *La Force de l'âge* which, among
other things, is a remarkable chronicle of the thirties
and especially of the war years as experienced by a
Parisian, it is accompanied by a minor theme: terror
before the inevitable end. Writing in 1960, Beauvoir
notes that for someone who, like herself, has always
lived in a privileged economic state, life contains two
truths that must be confronted simultaneously—"the
joy of living and the horror of having it end."[10]
Indeed, one of the most striking features of her work
is that beneath all the brisk activity, all the political
and intellectual commitment, all the optimism, there
runs a current of anxiety, a constant awareness of
death and of a finality that reduces our endeavors to
nothingness.

Beauvoir had her first intimation of nothingness
when she was a young girl. She relates the incident
in fictionalized form in her first published novel and
refers to it again, underlining its importance, in *Mémoires d'une jeune fille rangée*. Alone in her grandparents' house, she noticed her old worn jacket hang-
ing on the back of a chair. Suddenly it occurred to
her that the jacket was unable to say: "I'm an old
worn jacket." Terrified, the child saw in the jacket's
inertness and unconsciousness, above all in its inability
to mold thoughts into words, a glimpse of her own

eventual extinction. Trying to repress the notion of death, she ran out into the sunny garden where her family was assembled, and embraced life.

During her childhood and adolescence she occasionally had other intimations of death (whose speechlessness will always seem particularly terrifying to the often verbose Beauvoir), but they were quickly muffled by the hum of daily living and by preparations for the future. On her nineteenth birthday she sat in the library at the Sorbonne and wrote a long dialogue in which both voices, she says, were her own: the first proclaimed the vanity of all things and chanted a litany of disgust and fatigue; the second affirmed the beauty of existence.[11] Indeed, both voices weave through her work, the second usually dominant, the first adding a darker coloring to her thought.

In *La Force de l'âge* Beauvoir frequently refers to a schizophrenic streak in her nature. She defines her "schizophrenia" as a tendency to pursue her projects against all odds rather than adapting them to reality and to the realm of possibility. Furthermore, she saw in this tendency "an extreme and aberrant form of my optimism."[12] Having installed herself and Sartre at the center of the world, she imagined that around them revolved "people who were odious, ridiculous, or amusing, and who did not have eyes with which to observe me. I alone had the gift of sight."[13] She was the subject, the creative intelligence that bestowed life on those she deigned to favor with a glance; all others were objects.

No doubt the egotism which the then fifty-year-old Beauvoir discerns in the twenty-five-year-old woman she once was corresponds to something very real in her attitude during the thirties. In 1966 she told an interviewer that she viewed her life as a gradual and continual opening up to other people. She also affirmed, however, that at first, as one struggles to make one's way, a certain self-centeredness is healthy and desirable.

Beauvoir's repeated statements about her tendency in the thirties to exclude the majority of the human race from the luminous circle in which she and Sartre resided are not only comments about her own temperament; they are also, perhaps even primarily, ironic statements about the bourgeoisie. Although in the 1930s she thought that she had repudiated the bourgeois mentality, she later accuses herself of having embraced what she sees as its fundamental tenet—an aggressive individualism that excludes any meaningful concern for others. In her portrayal of herself in the decade before World War II, she underlines heavily, perhaps excessively, the egocentric nature of her apolitical stance, succumbing to a tendency to dramatize the difference between her prewar, individualistic attitude and her postwar attitude of collective guilt and responsibility for worldwide social inequities.

As she recalls those insouciant years prior to 1939, she sees in them a "golden age"[14] during which her principal function was to construct her own happiness. She no doubt indulges her taste for dramatization and exaggeration when she says that during those years she and Sartre were "elves," miraculously immune to the common fate of mankind. Sartre's *La Nausée* would suggest that he, at least, was of a different opinion. As Girard astutely points out, *La Force de l'âge* is, in many respects, an *Anti-Nausea*.[15]

After 1939, however, life ceased to be a game and, although she would always continue to live the privileged life of a bourgeois, she no longer simply *accepted* her situation; rather, she tried to *assume* it.

The nicety of the distinction between passively accepting one's situation and actively assuming it is perhaps not immediately evident to readers who are faced with the practical matters of living. For Beauvoir, however, it is a crucial distinction.

During the thirties Beauvoir wrote two novels which she never submitted to a publisher, and a collection of short stories ironically entitled *Primauté du spirituel* (Primacy of the Spiritual), which was rejected by the publishing house of Grasset. Eager to write ever since childhood, she had considerable difficulty in finding a subject. The reason, she explains, is that she was essentially too happy to have anything to say:

Literature appears when something in life goes out of whack. In order to write, the essential condition is that reality no longer be taken for granted. Only then is one able to perceive it and make it visible to others. Emerging from the boredom and bondage of my childhood years, I was overwhelmed, stunned, blinded with joy. How could I have found in my happiness an urge to escape from it? My plans for work remained empty dreams until the day when my happiness was threatened, and I rediscovered in solitude a certain kind of anxiety.[16]

Curiously, Beauvoir, who said that psychology was not her strong point and who, like Sartre, distrusted Freudian thought because it threatens the autonomy and supremacy of the consciousness, defines creativity in terms similar to those used by psychoanalytical critics. They too tend to see art as defense, as substitute, as reparation, although in the 1960s and 1970s psychoanalysis has begun to accept the notion that creativity may have roots in satisfaction as well as in a loss that needs repair or a wound that requires healing.

However that may be, Beauvoir's statement is

important; it indicates what she, at least, considers to be the source of her literary creativity. "After the declaration of war," she notes, "things finally ceased to be a matter of course. Unhappiness had erupted into the world. Literature became as necessary to me as the air I breathed."[17] In other words, Beauvoir's incessant rage against the inevitable misfortunes that are inherent in the human condition (especially old age and death) as well as her fulminations against miseries such as poverty, oppression, and hunger that are the lot of a high percentage of today's world population stoke up her creative imagination and compel her to write. Happy, she is sterile; indignant, she can write. Her indignation and her violent hatreds may perhaps be viewed not so much as an expression of feelings that exist prior to the act of writing, but as the only emotional mode that can sustain her creative drive. Since 1939 Beauvoir has cultivated a sense of outrage; it is the *sine qua non* of much of her literary work.

During the thirties, then, Beauvoir had difficulty in channeling her creative energies because, on the whole, she lived "in the implacable light of an unfailing happiness. For me it was quite a stupefying experience to learn how it feels to be sad,"[18] she notes. The experience of sadness to which she here refers was the result of the curious triangular relationship she and Sartre formed with Olga, one of Beauvoir's students. Moody and anticonformist, Olga fascinated both Beauvoir and Sartre. They saw in her a certain youthful contempt for the established order of things. At Sartre's insistence—Beauvoir is quite plain on this point—Olga, who was nine years younger than Beauvoir, was admitted to the magic circle that had heretofore contained only the two of them. Having tended to think that she and Sartre were but a single personality, Beauvoir was now forced to face up to the existence of another consciousness that began to play a vital role in her own life and that threatened her autonomy. "Olga forced me to confront a truth which hitherto, as I have said, I had made every effort to avoid—namely, that other people existed, exactly as I did, and that their existence was in every way as justified as mine."[19]

As might have have been predicted, the trio was not a resounding success. Eventually Olga drifted away from the other two. It lasted long enough though for Beauvoir to experience solitude and anxiety. It also provided her with the subject of a novel and, interrupting her happiness, it made it possible for her to transform the essence of a personal experience into a literary work of considerable interest. Although she says that she had begun *L'Invitée* before the failure of the ill-fated trio, this experience provided her with a stunning illustration of the novel's basic theme—a theme of primordial importance in Beauvoir's work: that is, the relationship of self with others, or to express it somewhat differently, the notion that for each individual the "original curse"[20] is the existence of others.

L'Invitée (She Came to Stay) was published in 1943. Sartre, who had been mobilized in 1939 and taken prisoner in Lorraine on June 21, 1940, had managed to get himself released on April 1, 1941 when the Germans freed some of their prisoners for work on the land. He had returned to Paris and during the war years both he and Beauvoir continued to teach philosophy in Parisian lycées. Although they sympathized with the Resistance movement and were no doubt deeply moved when they learned that certain of their friends had died in concentration camps or been killed in combat, they themselves lived in relative safety.

Begun before the outbreak of the war, *L'Invitée* opens with an epigraph by Hegel: "Each consciousness seeks the death of the other." Even though Beauvoir did not come upon Hegel's statement until she had already done considerable work on her novel, it neatly expresses the book's underlying metaphysical theme. The novel's strength is precisely the manner in which Beauvoir manages to give this abstract theme sensuous form and to incarnate it in the lives of her three principal protagonists.

In addition to illustrating one of the metaphysical themes that runs through existentialist thought, *L'Invitée* is, in the best tradition of the French psychological novel, a study of the devastating effects of love and jealousy.

The first scene takes place in the autumn of 1938. Although the novel chronicles the increasingly complicated emotional dilemmas of a man and two women, discreet allusions to the darkening political scene and to the ever more menacing threat of catastrophe heighten the sense of inevitability and impending doom. The book concludes shortly after the outbreak of hostilities in the autumn of 1939.

As the novel opens, Françoise, a writer, is working late at night in a darkened theater. She is finishing her adaptation of Shakespeare's *Julius Caesar* which Pierre Labrousse, a distinguished actor and director who is her long-time lover, plans to stage. Seated in her tiny office, Françoise is the center of a little circle in which the air is rose with human warmth and light. "Beyond, was the theater, inhuman and black."[21] On the first page of her novel and in a few crisp sentences, Beauvoir has thus suggested Françoise's relationship with the world: perfectly self-contained, she resides at the luminous center of being; the world outside her purview is black and inhuman; only when objects or other people, graced by a glance from her, register on her consciousness do they emerge from inchoate night and nothingness. Indeed, the first sentence of the novel is: "Françoise looked up."

Leaving her office on the pretext that she would like a drink of the whiskey that is in Pierre's dressing room, but in actual fact feeling drawn to the dark corridors, Françoise moves out into the theater, bringing it to life by her conscious awareness of it.

When she was not there, the smell of dust, the half-light, the forlorn solitude, all this did not exist for anyone; it did not exist at all. Now that she was there, the red of the carpet gleamed through the darkness like a timid night-light. She had the power to draw things from their inanimate state by her presence. It was as if she had been entrusted with a mission—to bring to life this theater, empty and filled with darkness.[22]

Stepping out into the night air, she exults in the realization that everything is asleep, inert, and that only she is conscious. "Nothing," the author comments, "was real except her own life."[23] Other people —their thoughts as well as their words and faces— are, as Françoise explains, simply objects that exist in her world. Her relationship with others is dominated by her strong sense of possessiveness and by her tendency to consider others as satellites that move in invariable and preordained orbits around herself, the sun.

Since the publication of Beauvoir's autobiography, it is apparent that much of *L'Invitée* is derived from the author's own experience. Françoise's attitude is precisely that of young Simone who, walking in the

country, felt that nature existed only because she was
there to see it and that God had charged her with
the mission of creating His world by looking at it.
Indeed, Françoise continues to dream Simone's childhood "dream of being my own cause and my own
end."[24]

The basically infantile nature of Françoise's
vision is obscured by the fact that she is in many ways
a mature, active, and highly intelligent woman. Like
all of Beauvoir's heroines, she is in love. At the beginning of the novel, she and Pierre form a happy couple
that has managed to create and maintain a relationship which, in Beauvoir's existentialist perspective,
passes for "authentic love." Working together on a
common project, they share the same aspirations. With
an exhilarating sense of comradeship, they fashion
their common future. Essentially they are partners.

This kind of love is the antithesis of *amour-
passion*. It is far removed from the concept of love as
a fatality—a notion that is supremely expressed in
the medieval tale of *Tristan and Isolde* and that has
colored much of Western man's thoughts about love.
(In *Le Deuxième Sexe* or *The Second Sex*, Beauvoir
summarily dismisses the view of love exemplified in
Tristan and Isolde, calling it "outmoded.")

Although Françoise and Pierre believe that theirs
is a perfect love, the relationship between them contains an ontological flaw that is as yet undetected but
that will gradually be exposed throughout the course
of the novel. One of the curious features of Beauvoir's
work as a whole is that the dogmatic and sometimes
oversimplified assertions in her sociological or polemical studies are often contradicted by her novels.
In the former she establishes theoretical positions and,
marshaling her considerable intellectual powers, defends them forcefully. In the latter she evokes, to use

her phrase, the opaqueness of contingency, that is to say, the ambiguities of life as experienced emotionally.

Thus, the kind of love that is called authentic in *Le Deuxième Sexe*—a love which somewhat resembles the "generous friendship (*amitié généreuse*) that characterizes the love of Cornelian heroes—is a freely chosen partnership of two autonomous beings who share a common goal and hold each other in the highest esteem. In *L'Invitée*, however, this type of love is shown as being illusory for two basic reasons: seeing the relationship between people as one of hostility, Beauvoir illustrates the existentialist view that each consciousness affirms its autonomy and liberty by active opposition to every other consciousness (the metaphysical motif of the novel), thus making of Françoise's and Pierre's supposed oneness a momentary illusion; secondly, although existentialism, in theory at least, tends to adopt the Cartesian separation of mind and body and so assures autonomy for the consciousness, Beauvoir's novels tend to show characters—especially female characters—who react emotionally, at times even hysterically, when confronted with personal problems and dilemmas (the psychological aspect of the novel).

Beauvoir's female protagonists are in fact patterned after their creator. A reader of Beauvoir's autobiography cannot help but be struck by the author's emotionalism and by her fits of weeping at moments of joy or sorrow. Furthermore, Beauvoir's dependence on Sartre is reflected in the need of her female characters to see themselves mirrored in the eyes of a man. Here again the view of love expressed in *Le Deuxième Sexe*, with its insistence on a woman's independence, is at variance with the experience of love conveyed in the novels. Françoise feels as if her life is secure and somehow justified by the presence of Pierre. She is in fact totally dependent on him. "Every moment of her life that she entrusted to Pierre was given back to her, clear, polished, perfected, and became a moment of their shared life."[25]

This is precisely Beauvoir's attitude toward Sartre. In *Mémoires d'une jeune fille rangée* she explains that in her youth her need to admire someone was unfulfilled because she knew no one who was worthy of the devotion she felt capable of giving. Then she met Sartre. For her, Sartre's very existence justified the world, although she notes that for Sartre there was nothing that could justify the world.[26] Commenting on Beauvoir's attitude, critic Elaine Marks observes, a bit tartly perhaps: "What Simone de Beauvoir is in fact saying is God is dead; long live Sartre."[27] In her famous and combative analysis of "the second sex," Beauvoir fails to come to grips with this feminine need (it is she in her novels who depicts it as such) to cling to a man and to have one or more passionate love affairs—a need that is central to her own life and to that of her heroines.

Contrary to what Françoise and Pierre believe at the beginning of *L'Invitée*, their love is essentially a product of language. Their communion is basically verbal. In fact, Françoise can sense her own existence only by translating her experiences into words for Pierre. "Nothing was completely real until she had told Pierre about it. Otherwise, it was almost as if it had never existed at all."[28]

When Pierre and Françoise decide to take in hand the young Xavière, who wants to escape the stifling provincial atmosphere of Rouen, they gradually discover two truths: the metaphysical truth that each consciousness is autonomous and hostile to every other consciousness, and the psychological truth that they are not pure minds but human beings who possess bodies and complex emotions and who are consumed by jealousy and unsatisfied desires.

Xavière is, then, a kind of catalyst. That Françoise and Pierre invite her to live with them may strike the reader as surprising, for she seems to be, as critic Maurice Cranston put it, "a charmless bitch."[29] Beauvoir remarks in her own analysis of the novel (she discusses each of her works in her autobiography) that by setting the story in Paris and by giving Françoise and Pierre active careers and very busy lives she reduced considerably the credibility of their interest in Xavière. Only the lack of distraction in a provincial town and the boredom of, say, two young lycée professors of philosophy could, she notes, explain their passionate, almost maniacal, desire to make of Xavière a carbon copy of themselves.

Still, even without the background of a small town, the novel has a decidedly claustrophobic atmosphere. Most of it consists of long and inconclusive conversations among the three protagonists (either together or in couples) that take place in Françoise's room, Xavière's room, backstage in the theater, or—and this is the most frequent setting—in any of three or four dark, smoky bars or nightclubs in Montparnasse. Huddled around a tiny table, they spend hours —usually from midnight to dawn—analyzing each other's words, gestures, and glances.

Beauvoir's reaction against her proper background is such that somber bars, especially those that are haunted by pariahs and down-and-outers, exert an endless fascination on her and, in contrast to the hated tea rooms for elderly spinsters, seem like temples of truth. She often flaunts her fondness for a certain grubbiness and sordidness. During her four-month stay in the United States in 1947, she visited cheap bars that were frequented by derelicts, and went into flophouses on Chicago's West Madison Avenue. Escorted by Nelson Algren, her Chicago host, into a particularly dingy saloon in which the men, covered with vermin, were lying on the floor, Beauvoir, in a gush of rapturous pleasure, exclaimed excitedly in English: "It is beautiful."[30]

Moody and unpredictable, Xavière has a mysterious, elusive quality that alternately exasperates and intrigues both Françoise and Pierre. Seen only through the eyes of the other characters, she evades the reader as much as she does them. She is, as the author remarks, "a living question mark,"[31] for she incarnates the opaqueness of a consciousness closed in on itself.

Pierre, too, is something of a question mark. Beauvoir herself notes that in general she had greater success with her female characters than with her male characters. In the case of Pierre, she explains, she did not wish to pattern him too directly after Sartre. Seen essentially through the admiring eyes of Françoise, he has Sartre's creative energy, generosity, and strong personality, but he remains rather abstract and seems more like a caricature than a real person.

Beauvoir's refusal to present authorial analyses of her protagonists and her reliance on dialogue to reveal the psychological motivation of her characters are a result of her concept of the novel, which in turn has its roots in her philosophical position concerning appearance and reality. Like Sartre, she rejects the traditional view, particularly strong in thinkers of Neoplatonic persuasion, that there is a difference between appearance and innermost reality, between the exterior world and our inner life, between our words, our glances, our acts, and our secret being. Supporting her argument by references to Hegel, Beauvoir affirms that the real must never be conceived as an interiority hidden behind external appearances. The exterior hides nothing; rather it expresses.[32]

But since appearances are subject to endless interpretations, it follows that reality is never fixed. It is ambiguous and multiple. Contrary to her philosophical works which set forth opinions clearly, the novels express ambiguities, doubts, and hesitations. Technically this is achieved by telling the story from different points of view. Although Beauvoir would use this device much more extensively in her second novel, she already tried it out in her first, and discovered that it conveyed successfully the feeling of a multiple and dense, at times, almost impenetrable reality.

Around the trio move a dozen or so characters, each with his own life that tangentially touches one or more of the three principal protagonists but that is independent of their lives. The most interesting of them is Elizabeth, Pierre's sister who is the first of Beauvoir's women to love hopelessly and servilely, that is to say, inauthentically. She is the mistress of a man to whom she is passionately attached. A would-be playwright, her lover hopes that through her influence Pierre will be cajoled into producing his latest play (ironically entitled *Partage* or *Sharing*), which is execrable. He has told Elizabeth for several years that he is going to divorce his wife and, although she no longer believes him, she has nothing to live for but this vain hope. Her life is characterized by suffering and hypocrisy. Even her mediocre career as a painter is built on deception because she knows only too well that she has no real talent for painting.

When, during one of their interminable conversations, Françoise hears Pierre say to Xavière: "We who have so much respect for you . . . ,"[33] she suddenly rebels against being included in that "we," for she does not at that moment have much respect for Xavière. Feeling that Pierre has no right to speak in her name, she dimly senses for the first time that they are not one. As her malaise increases, she feels less and less sure of her relationship with Pierre, indeed, of her relationship with Xavière. What at first had seemed clear now becomes cloudy. One wintry night when Pierre and Xavière go out walking in the snow, Françoise suddenly perceives them as enemies who have abandoned her "without hope, in the heart of emptiness and chaos."[34]

Unable to remain alone in her room, she goes out and climbs the narrow streets, snowy and silent, that lead to the top of Montmartre. Having lived entirely in conjunction with Pierre and now feeling abandoned by him, she feels as if she has no existence whatsoever. Her crisis of consciousness is played out against a background of night and chilling cold. As she starts to walk home she suddenly realizes that she has a fever and is indeed ill.

Her illness is both an escape from the ineluctable truth that she is "a naked consciousness confronting the world"[35] and an interlude in the evolution of the novel. Suffering from a pulmonary infection, she is forced to spend several weeks in a clinic and then in her room. Pampered and passive, she reverts at first to the privileged state of childhood in which everything is automatically provided. Recovering slowly, she passes from childhood back to adulthood—a state in which, Beauvoir remarks elsewhere, "everything must be built and conquered."[36]

The situation to which she returns after her recovery is somewhat different from the one just prior to her illness. During her absence, Pierre and Xavière have had time to draw closer together. Xavière, however, has resisted being annexed to Pierre's world the

way Françoise had been. It is precisely this resistance
that intrigues and exasperates Pierre, for he, like
Françoise, is possessive and finds it difficult to accept
the idea that someone as seemingly flaccid and in-
significant as Xavière might oppose his will. In-
stinctively trying to form an alliance with Xavière
against Pierre, Françoise, too, encounters obstinancy
and refusal on the part of the girl she mistakenly
thinks "belongs" to her, but who is, decidedly, "an
alien, rebellious consciousness."[37]

Having failed to make of Xavière a docile accomplice, Pierre and Françoise turn to one another
and spend hours talking about Xavière. Certain critics
have asserted that Beauvoir's forte is dialogue. Others
have maintained that her weakness as a novelist is
her inability to write credible dialogue. It is no doubt
true that *L'Invitée*, like most but not all of her novels,
is too long. Beauvoir's desire to "tell all" has not
always stood her in good stead.

Then too, her dialogue, which is finely articulated
and neatly phrased, tends to be highly stylized. Noting
that she wished to imitate and not copy the kind of
speech she heard around her, Beauvoir says that a
good novelist never reproduces the stammerings of a
real conversation.[38] The dialogue in *L'Invitée* is in
harmony with the overall stylization of the novel.

The theme of the novel is made explicit—probably
too explicit—in a conversation between Pierre and
Françoise. "You're the only person I know," says
Pierre, "who bursts into tears on discovering in someone else a consciousness similar to your own. Everyone
experiences his own consciousness as an absolute. How
can several absolutes be compatible? The problem is
as great a mystery as life or death. What surprised me
is that you should be affected in such a concrete way
by a metaphysical situation."[39] Françoise remarks that

only when she met Xavière did she realize that her "consciousness was not unique in the world,"[40] a statement which underlines the metaphysical theme but which, from a psychological point of view, makes Françoise seem absurdly naïve and immature. Unable to accept the notion that Xavière exists as autonomously as she, Françoise feels that she must kill her rival.

Throughout all her work, Beauvoir tends to view the self as inescapably locked in conflict with others. In *L'Invitée* this enmity is shown as being derived from the very nature of consciousness itself. After drawing closer to Marxist ideology, Beauvoir will see the struggle between the self and others, not so much in ontological terms as in terms of a class conflict based on economic realities. Both explanations, however, originate in the perception of man as a creature driven by predatory instincts. Later in life, she will believe that her view of interpersonal relationships has become somewhat less dogmatic, although she will insist that "on the political level, I remain Manichean."[41] Indeed, Beauvoir has always tended to divide mankind into two opposing camps: "adversaries and allies"[42] the two fundamental categories through which she seems to grasp experience. She has remarked that "we always work for certain people against others."[43] The adversaries and the allies differ from book to book, but the two categories remain constant, giving her world its basic order.

Beauvoir has both criticized and defended the ending of *L'Invitée*. When war breaks out in September, 1939, Pierre leaves for the front. Françoise and Xavière now confront each other directly with no possibility of soliciting support from a third party. Françoise feels that Xavière's existence is an intolerable threat to her own autonomy. Seeing in Xavière the incarnation of a consciousness that is totally self-contained, Françoise feels excluded, indeed annihilated —as if she were reduced to the state of an inert object, of nothingness. Unable to endure "this enemy presence"[44] any longer, she opens the gas spigot in Xavière's room, destroying not only her rival for Pierre's attentions, but also her intimations of her own nothingness. Like Corneille's Medea who exults in her crime because she sees in it proof of her ability to determine her own fate, Françoise says to herself jubilantly: "I have done it of my own free will." And in the closing lines of the novel, the author comments: "It was her own will which was being fulfilled. Now nothing separated her from herself. At last she had chosen. She had chosen herself."[45]

Beauvoir's original title for the novel was *Légitime Défense* (Legitimate Defense). She defends the murder at the end by saying that it is the logical and ultimate conclusion of the metaphysical theme announced in Hegel's epigraph. However, she admits that psychologically it is less defensible because Françoise, as depicted throughout the novel, would have been incapable of such an act. But psychological and aesthetic concerns were not dominant in Beauvoir's mind as she wrote the final scene. For her, Xavière's murder had a cathartic value. By killing Olga on paper she got rid of the irritation and resentment she might have felt toward her. More importantly, however, by releasing Françoise, through the agency of a crime, from the dependent position in which her love for Pierre had kept her, Beauvoir felt that she had regained her own personal autonomy.[46] Although the conclusion might appear hasty and awkward, the death of Olga-cum-Xavière was, she explains, the driving force and the raison d'être of the whole novel. Thus *L'Invitée* incarnates a personal dilemma which is resolved by means of literature.

It is, however, probably a mistake to read Beauvoir's novels as if they were principally novels of ideas, containing a philosophical content which, like a lode of ore, must be extracted even at the expense of ruining the surface texture. At their best, they are evocations of a concrete, living reality. Concerned with the dense and shifting texture of existence, Beauvoir dramatizes in *L'Invitée* the difficulty of living and the walled-in or claustrophobic quality of human experience. In addition to its often subtle psychological portrayal, the novel contains finely articulated scenes that evoke, among other things, a first night at the theater and the curious human fauna that frequented out-of-the-way Parisian bars in the thirties. Occasionally verbose, often delicately ironic and densely poetic, *L'Invitée* is one of Beauvoir's best books.

Appearing during the bleak days of the war and in the same year as Sartre's *L'Être et le néant* (*Being and Nothingness*) as well as his *Les Mouches* (*The Flies*), *L'Invitée* was well received. Beauvoir had worked on it since 1938; in 1941 it had been accepted by Gallimard. By 1943 she felt that she had already gone beyond the "individualist" concerns that had characterized her thinking in the thirties and that were embodied in *L'Invitée*. She was already preoccupied with the ethical and moral problems which would be her special contribution to existentialism, leaving pure philosophical speculation to Sartre. In fact, she had already finished her second novel which, because it was set in occupied France, she knew could not be published until after the war.

In 1939, with the outbreak of war, she had discovered, so she says, "human solidarity, my responsibilities, and the fact that it is possible to accept death so that life might keep its meaning. But," she adds, "I learned these truths more or less against my natural inclinations. I used words to talk myself into accepting them. I explained them to myself, I turned my powers of persuasion inward and preached them to myself."[47] In short, she entered what she calls her "moral phase."[48] Benefiting from Sartre's fame and having proved that she was a writer of distinction in her own right, she left her teaching post in 1943 (Sartre would do the same in 1945), and henceforth devoted herself entirely to literature.

3

Ethics

and the

Moral Phase

In 1943 Beauvoir agreed to contribute an essay to a projected series of volumes dealing with recent trends in philosophy. Her second but as yet unpublished novel (*Le Sang des autres* or *The Blood of Others*) had touched on a number of questions which she wished to develop more fully. Thus the essay, which turned out to be a small book, is closely associated with the novel. Published in 1944 under the title of *Pyrrhus et Cinéas* (Pyrrhus and Cyneas), it is a popularization of existentialist thought which had just recently been expounded in Sartre's massive and as yet not widely known study on being and nothingness.

The title of her book refers to an anecdote related by Plutarch and recounted by Beauvoir in the opening page of her essay. Pyrrhus, king of Epirus, one day enumerated to his counselor, Cinéas, the lands he intended to conquer. When Cinéas asked Pyrrhus what he planned to do after conquering India, the king answered: "Then I'll rest." "In that case," said Cinéas, "why don't you rest right away?"[1]

Beauvoir's essay is designed to show that Pyrrhus, not Cinéas, is right. Her method is essentially aphoristic rather than analytical. Somewhat like the famous French moralists of the seventeenth and eighteenth centuries, Beauvoir asserts beliefs and opinions in the form of maxims and *sententiae* which are arresting but often are debatable.

Along with Sartre, Beauvoir had been profoundly impressed by Husserl's remark that consciousness is consciousness of something. She notes that man is therefore constitutionally oriented toward something other than himself. Man is defined as transcendence, as movement toward something outside himself, as project; or, as Heidegger remarked in a phrase that Beauvoir cites in several of her works: "Man is a creature of distances."[2] He strives toward a goal, but as soon as he attains it, the goal falls into the past and becomes a point of departure. Since man is a projection toward the future, he can find happiness only in transcending the present, which is continually slipping into the past. There is perhaps more than a little romanticism in Beauvoir's celebration of man's restless spirit and his desire for experience. Her remarks echo, but in a different register, Faust's cry as he discovers that in the midst of enjoyment he yearns, never satisfied, for new desire:

Thus I reel from desire to satisfaction,
And in satisfaction long for desire.[3]

Pleasure, Beauvoir suggests, is not in repose. Like Nietzsche, who was himself strongly marked by Faustian aspirations and who proclaimed that joy is found only in battle, Beauvoir declares that renunciation of struggling is tantamount to renunciation of transcendence, of being itself. Man's being is not the fixed, immutable being of things. "The paradox of the human condition," she explains, "is in the fact that every goal can be transcended; and yet, in terms of the project, the goal is defined as a final point; in order to transcend the goal one must first have projected it as something that cannot be transcended."[4] There is no other way for man to exist, Beauvoir affirms.

Pyrrhus et Cinéas is divided into two parts. In the first, Beauvoir condemns those who advocate an epicurean enjoyment of the moment in the mistaken belief that a moment can be seized and fixed. The moment can only be enjoyed if, paradoxically, it is rejected in favor of a future that is as yet unattained. The attitude suggested in Horace's famous phrase, *Carpe diem*, and for example, in Gide's early novel, *Les Nourritures terrestres (Fruits of the Earth)*, is false and can only lead to boredom. Beauvoir also rejects any attempt to arrive at the infinite, whether it be called God or Humanity. A man's projects must be finite, for if he attempts to transcend the finite he loses all sense of his own identity and singularity. He loses his being.

As always in her thought, Beauvoir makes a sharp distinction between man, proud possessor of a consciousness, and the rest of the world. She alludes to Sartre's demonstration in *L'Être et le néant* that "the being of man is not the immutable being of things."[5] One might argue that the belief that man is radically different from the world around him borders on arrogance. It belongs to an era that is not so distant in time but that predates general ecological awareness. Like Sartre, Beauvoir is contemptuous of science and disdainfully rejects any data that might threaten the supremacy of man's consciousness, of his subjective awareness of self. She dismisses pantheism as a phase through which young girls sometimes pass. She dislikes animals and refuses to see any kinship or fundamental bond between them and mankind.

Formulated during the years of the German occupation, existentialism was marked by the climate of crisis that prevailed in France in the late thirties and especially in the early forties. Striving aggressively to preserve the dignity of the thinking self, Beauvoir expounded a doctrine that relegated to the category of otherness (*altérité*) everything outside the lucid and independent self. The subjective nature of existentialism has been criticized by, among others, the famous anthropologist Lévi-Strauss, who had known Beauvoir and Sartre during the thirties: "The intellectual current that was going to flower into existentialism seemed to me to be the opposite of a valid mode of thought, mainly because of its complacency toward the illusions of subjectivity. This elevation of personal preoccupations to the dignified level of philosophical problems runs the serious risk of ending up as a kind of metaphysics for working girls."[6] Beauvoir was later to criticize the subjectivism (the word is hers) she discerned in *Pyrrhus et Cinéas*.

In the second part of her essay she tries to establish some positive ethical principles and accepts Sartre's notion of freedom and choice—the fundamental postulate in existentialism: "Whatever the circumstances, we have a freedom of action that enables us to surmount them."[7] However, she calls attention to Descartes' distinction between our freedom and our power, between what depends on us and what does not. Man therefore "is free in situation,"[8] a notion she adopted, of course, from Sartre. External forces and other people can obviously impose certain limits on the exercise of our freedom. Still, we can realize our being only by making free choices within our particular situation. Each of our choices then becomes an act for which we are responsible in the eyes of others.

Despite her recognition of the existence of others and of their freedom which is as absolute as hers, Beauvoir in *Pyrrhus et Cinéas* tends to present the individual as achieving his own transcendence by using the collectivity of which he is inevitably a part as if it were a kind of convenient instrument. She later re-examined her essay from the vantage point of Marxism and denounced this "individualist tendency."[9] Many readers, however, have found her defense of man's freedom—austere and demanding as it is since it implies unlimited responsibility—more exhilarating and tonic than her later tendency to toe the Marxist line and to indulge uncritically in left-wing cant.

There are novels which, because of an intricate design or an extensive and radical use of ellipses, must be read twice to be fully comprehended. Few novels require a second reading as urgently as *Le Sang des autres*, 1945 (*The Blood of Others*). The difficulty lies not in the narrative line, which is basically simple, but in the manner in which Beauvoir constructs the novel. Impressed by Dos Passos, Faulkner, and other American writers, she wished to experiment with form in an attempt to evoke the dense, shifting, ambiguous texture of life. To achieve this end she tells her story from different points of view. The unheralded shifts from one point of view to another mean that a reader does not know at first who is speaking, to whom the personal pronouns refer, and whether the narrative is being related by the author or through the consciousness of a particular character.

Gradually, however, the voices become recognizable. Characters emerge, and the reader becomes aware of the fact that the confusion and indeterminateness which he felt in the opening pages is the calculated effect of a skillful writer who wishes to express the complexity of existence.

At the beginning of the novel, the thirty-some-year-old Jean Blomart is seated at the bedside of his dying mistress, Hélène. The setting is occupied Paris during World War II. It is night. (Much of *L'Invitée* also took place at night.) Hélène has been fatally wounded while on a sabotage mission undertaken on behalf of the Resistance movement of which Blomart is a group leader. In the next room, his friends are waiting for him to give the order for another mission. His decision must be made by 6 A.M. On the final page of the novel, Hélène dies, and Blomart gives the order to proceed as planned.

Within the five or six hours Blomart sits by Hélène's bedside, he confronts his entire past, modifying and reshaping it in light of the present and of the singularly ominous future. The past, which is now experienced retrospectively, is thus contained within an urgent present. Reconstructing events that have led up to the present moment, Blomart refers to himself in the first person when he identifies with the boy and young man he once was and in the third person when he describes himself as he appeared in the eyes of others. Thoughts and emotions specifically provoked by Hélène's imminent death or by the decision he must soon make periodically interrupt the chronological flow of the narrative and are printed in italics. Alternating with Blomart's retelling of his life is the account of Hélène's life, narrated in the third person.

The novel begins with an epigraph taken from Dostoevski's *The Brothers Karamazov*: "Everyone is responsible to everybody for everything." The book itself is both an illustration of this dictum and an anxious examination of the validity of Dostoevski's sweeping statement. The tone is relentlessly earnest as the characters grapple with the tortuous problems of guilt and responsibility.

Le Sang des autres adds an ethical dimension to the metaphysical and (since in the last resort all metaphysics is rooted in psychology) psychological themes dealt with in *L'Invitée*. Françoise's murder of Xavière is clearly an impractical solution to the problems posed by the self's necessary coexistence with others. It is valid only as a symbolic gesture in Françoise's private world. After 1939, a larger world impinged on Beauvoir's consciousness and she wished to paint on a bigger canvas, to communicate with a reality which, in her drive for a purely personal happiness, she had by and large ignored—the world of politics and economics, of war, crime and death.

Son of a well-to-do printer, Blomart was brought

up in a bourgeois milieu and was destined to follow
in his father's footsteps. At the age of eight he discovered the "scandal" of death: the infant son of a
former maid died, and young Blomart was disconso-
late.[10] Cunningly, Beauvoir associates the boy's anguished awareness of death with his equally distressing
awareness of the fact that he belongs to an economically privileged class. As a child and as an adolescent,
Blomart was continually haunted by a sense of guilt
and by a pervasive feeling of remorse. Indeed, the
notion of remorse (*remords*) informs much of the novel
and is elaborated in richly metaphorical language.

On the one hand remorse is associated with the
comfortably appointed apartment in which the Blo-
marts live and which is located above the press shop.
When the family goes to the country for a holiday,
Jean is no longer troubled by remorse. Back in the
apartment, however, he senses its insidious presence
among the silk cushions, lovely rugs, fine crystal, and
beautiful flowers. It permeates his being, entering his
eyes, his ears, his nostrils. Like a criminal, it prowls
through the rooms. It is a "thick air" that seems to
creep up the stairs leading from the shop filled with
laboring workmen to the large apartment. It is a
malaise that filters through the rooms, profoundly
disturbing Jean, whose father and two sisters, however, seem to be unaware of its sinister presence.

On the other hand remorse, as well as being a
by-product of wealth, is also sensed as being inherent
in existence itself. Some of the complexities and ambiguities of *Le Sang des autres* result from the fact that
Beauvoir, although she clearly situates guilt and remorse in a socio-political context, also views them as
attributes of existence. As such, they become a metaphysical rather than a social or political problem.
"Crime is everywhere, irremediable, inexpiable," notes

Beauvoir authorially, "the crime of existing."[11] Contrasting with passages in which remorse seems to be contained within the walls of a bourgeois family's apartment, are numerous passages in which it seems to emanate from "the absolute rottenness hidden in the heart of every human destiny."[12] Commenting on "the corrupt odor of the world," Beauvoir writes: "It was not only the house; the whole city was infested with it; the whole world."[13]

The attitude of Jean's mother is significant because, although Jean rejects his father, he senses that his mother secretly repudiates capitalism, marriage, and other bourgeois values even though she continues to defend them. Her condemnation of change is explained by the fact that for her "evil does not reside in institutions, but in the innermost recesses of ourselves."[14] There is something decidedly Augustinian in this harsh vision of an evil force that is harbored within us and that we cannot eradicate. The teen-aged Jean seemingly rejects his mother's negativistic view and, wishing to see evil not within us but in our institutions, sets out to change the world so that there will be "no more war, no more unemployment, no more servile work, no more misery."[15] However, the course of his life shows that he did not succeed in changing the world. His somber meditations by Hélène's bedside seem to echo his mother's unspoken desperation as it dawns on him that "there is perhaps no solution."[16]

In *La Force de l'âge* Beauvoir criticizes *Le Sang des autres* harshly and, it seems to me, unjustly. The novel is too didactic, she says. Although twentieth-century Western aestheticians have by and large been contemptuous of didacticism in literature, it might be pointed out that much of the world's great literature of previous centuries contains a clearly didactic impulse. Furthermore, the accusation of didacticism sounds rather odd coming from Beauvoir, whose later works are often aggressively didactic and who condemns the *nouveau roman* for its social irrelevance.

Beauvoir's dissatisfaction with *Le Sang des autres* may well be due, in part at least, to the fact that after she had embraced Marxist explanations for the world's ills she tended to identify evil, guilt, and responsibility with a specific group of people and a specific economic system, that is to say, with the bourgeoisie and capitalism. In her later works, the enemy is clearly identified. Problems of guilt and responsibility, so tortuously complicated in *Le Sang des autres*, become grossly simplified. Often they are reduced to propagandistic clichés. Writing in 1972, for example, Beauvoir calmly and with scarcely concealed delight imagines a worldwide holocaust triggered by the collapse of the American economy and the utter destruction of American society—a prospect which friends told her was imminent. She concludes her radiant vision of "planetary revolution" with the comment: "I don't know if I shall live long enough to witness it, but it is a consoling thought."[17]

In her later years Beauvoir seems to suffer from the eternal illusion that if only a certain polluted race of men could be swept from the face of the earth all would be well. Critic François Bondy pinpointed accurately if somewhat mordantly this aspect of Beauvoir's political thought in the fifties and sixties: "Between the happiness of the abstract masses and the destruction of the abstract villains," he wrote apropos of Beauvoir, "humanity is reserved for a privileged few: one's own little circle."[18]

Given her later Marxist-oriented attitude Beauvoir may have felt uneasy while rereading *Le Sang des autres*. Although the bourgeoisie is here shown as being largely responsible for social and economic ills, existence (for which the bourgeoisie cannot be made responsible) is itself considered an ill, a "crime." Indeed, in *Le Sang des autres* bourgeois remorse is simply one variety of the all-pervasive remorse immanent in existence. That this almost Jansenist pessimism is the result of Beauvoir's reaction to the war is made clear in the last volume of her autobiography: "The dark side of my existence was never more opaque than during the war."[19] *Le Sang des autres* evokes precisely this opaqueness of existence, the sense of being entrapped, of submitting to existence rather than fashioning it.

Beauvoir's later analysis of her reaction to the war of some thirty years earlier is curious. "The truth became apparent to me in 1939,"[20] she notes in 1972. But the truth of which she is speaking is not the truth of human suffering; it is not even a political or social truth. It is the realization (embarrassingly naïve for a thirty-one-year-old woman) that she is not a completely autonomous, sovereign being in a world designed primarily for her benefit. "I came to the realization that I was living passively because I had ceased to accept willingly the circumstances which life imposed upon me. Every day, at every hour, I calculated the extent to which I was dependent on external events. The war overwhelmed me; it separated me from Sartre and cut me off from my sister. I went from fear to despair, then to anger and to a loathing that was occasionally alleviated by flashes of hope."[21] The rhetorical language and self-dramatization seem exaggerated, perhaps even tasteless, when one realizes that during most of the war (from June 1941 onward) Sartre, along with Beauvoir, lived in relative comfort in Paris and that Beauvoir had been separated from her sister for long intervals during the previous ten years. Be that as it may, Beauvoir evoked her somber mood during the war years far more convincingly in *Le Sang des autres* than in her pompous and simplistic comments written some thirty-odd years later.

Wishing to escape from the apartment with its "old smell of remorse"[22] and eager to move toward "future horizons where remorse would not prowl,"[23] Jean left home and joined the Communist party. Essentially he rejected as inauthentic a life he had not chosen. Unwilling to accept values that had been created by others, he illustrates the existentialist ethics of choice. He agitated vigorously for Communist causes until the day a younger friend, idealistic and full of enthusiasm, was killed at a political rally. Jean felt directly responsible for Jacques' death and withdrew from the party, devoting himself exclusively to trade-union activities. As fascism and totalitarianism swept across Europe in the 1930s, Jean remained resolutely pacifist. He attempted to avoid guilt by avoiding commitment and violence.

Jean discovered, of course, that choice cannot be eluded. Abstention is impossible because one's very existence impinges on that of others. Both what one does and what one refrains from doing affect others. Like Sartre, Beauvoir uses images of stickiness, of viscosity, to suggest the progressive entrapment of the self with others—an entrapment which is an inevitable condition of existence. "I wish that every human life might be pure transparent freedom," remarks Jean as he begins to realize that, whether he wills it or not, his very existence profoundly alters the lives of several people around him; "I gradually realized that in the lives of others I was an opaque barrier."[24]

Beauvoir's success in *Le Sang des autres*, as in *L'Invitée*, is not essentially in illustrating an abstract idea (which she does) but in evoking the increasing

heaviness, density, and solidification of existence
through an ever more complicated network of relationships among a limited number of protagonists.
In her second novel as in her first, the dilemma of
interpersonal relationships is revealed in its starkest,
most tragic form in love. Jean's realization that each
of his refusals as well as each of his acts—that is to
say, each of his choices—resonates in another being is
the result not so much of his political or trade-union
activities as of his relationship with Hélène.

Somewhat like Xavière, Hélène is ferociously self-
centered. But whereas Xaxière would spend all day
locked up in her airless room, seemingly content to do
nothing, Hélène desperately wants something to hap-
pen to her. She compares her existence to that of an
oyster, confined between two shells and sunk in a
mass of viscous, flaccid matter. Basically she lacks a
goal, a cause to which she can devote her energies and
through which she can justify her life. Beauvoir admits that she drew heavily on her own experience in
her portrayal of Hélène. Indeed, Hélène's description
of her youthful attitude toward God is exactly young
Simone's attitude as described in *Mémoires d'une
jeune fille rangée*. "When I was little," says Hélène,
"I believed in God. It was magnificent. Something
was demanded of me at every moment. It seemed to
me that I *had* to exist. It was an absolute necessity."[25]

The need to feel necessary, the attempt to justify
one's life by participation in an enterprise that one
defines as essential is a principal driving force in
Beauvoir's own life. A vociferous atheist, she is nevertheless a believer by upbringing and by temperament.
Literature itself is a salvation because "books intro-
duce into this deplorably meaningless, contingent
world a necessity which rebounds to the credit of the
author."[26] Equally significant is her statement, re-

peated several times in one form or another throughout her autobiography, that Sartre replaced God as
the guarantor of her security and that his presence
gave her life its inner cohesion and necessity: "I
trusted him so completely that he guaranteed me the
sort of absolute security formerly provided by my
parents or by God. When I threw myself into the
world of freedom, I found a cloudless sky above my
head. I was free from all constraints, and yet every
moment of my existence possessed its own inevitability, its own necessity."[27]

Hélène would like to find in Jean the same security, the same necessity she had previously found in
God. When Jean refuses her love, she gives herself to
the first man available. Three or four months later
she has an abortion, and Jean, illustrating the novel's
Dostoevskian epigraph, feels responsible for her unhappiness which, he realizes, is a direct consequence
of his rejection of her adoration. He learns that he is
not free to refuse Hélène's love. A reader may well
balk at this logic and think it unreasonable to make
Jean guilty of Hélène's pregnancy and abortion. Such,
however, is the novel's thesis. This is one of the very
few instances in which the psychological motivation
seems inadequate to sustain the abstract theme announced in the epigraph.

Just as Jean, before he began to love Hélène,
wished to keep the world at a distance, so Hélène,
now believing that only their love and happiness have
any meaning, denies any responsibility for social or
political conditions in the world around her. She
refuses to take any interest in the ominous political
events of the late 1930s. Eventually, however, circumstances overtake her, just as they had overtaken Jean.
One day when she sees Jewish children being deported
she realizes that refusal to act is itself a choice. She
asks to participate in acts of sabotage against the

Nazis, and it is during one such mission that she is mortally wounded.

Le Sang des autres is, among other things, one of the few fine novels about the Occupation and the Resistance. Only after the publication of *La Force de l'âge* in 1960 could a reader know to what extent the novel was based on Beauvoir's actual experiences. Several of its most notable scenes are related in a somewhat more journalistic mode in the autobiography. Among them is the superbly articulated account of Jean's (Sartre's) departure for the army and of Hélène's (Beauvoir's) later visit to him at the front. The pathos, the awkwardness, the confusion, and the helplessness that so often inform important moments in one's life are beautifully conveyed.

A number of other characters appear in the pages of the novel. Most important among them are Marcel and his mistress, Denise. Like Elizabeth in *L'Invitée*, Denise has abdicated her autonomy and tries to live her life through that of another—of Marcel, a young painter and sculptor. Desperately she wants him to become famous so that a reflection of his celebrity will fall on her, assuring her, she believes, of happiness. When she is eventually forced to recognize the fact that Marcel will never be famous, she makes a pathetic attempt to find her own identity. She writes a novel that is no more of an artistic success than were Elizabeth's paintings.

Beauvoir's portrayal of Marcel was inspired in part—but only in part—by the distinguished sculptor Giacometti (one of her friends) and by Giacometti's description of fellow artist Duchamp. Marcel began his career brilliantly. Denise's desire to be associated with a famous man seemed about to be realized. Suddenly Marcel abandoned painting, refused all commissions and spent his time cutting out figures in lumps of sugar and braiding string. Later he lay in bed all day and did nothing at all. Marcel's withdrawal from artistic activity parallels Jean's departure from the Communist party and subsequent pacifism. Not content with creating art that retains an imprint of the human spirit which fashioned it, Marcel dreams of a pure art, untarnished by traces of humanity. He would even like to create an art that could somehow dispense with the eye of an observer. His increasingly pathological aspiration toward an ideal that in fact denies the human and that therefore denies all art itself is the aesthetic equivalent of Jean's ethics of noncommitment.

Marcel's presence in *Le Sang des autres* permits Beauvoir to comment on art. Describing Marcel's work that was on display at his highly successful exposition early in the novel, she writes:

All the paintings were enclosed within themselves, sheltered from any consciousness. Statues without faces, men changed into salt, public squares burned with the fire of death, oceans caught in the immobility of a unique and pure instant—all were various forms of absence. And while the viewer contemplated this universe that was without witnesses, it seemed as if he were absent from himself, as if he were stationed outside his own life in an empty and white eternity.[28]

Art is here seen as "a dream of purity and absence."[29] Beauvoir would later jettison this notion of art which, in her view, is contaminated with irresponsible bourgeois idealism and aestheticism, just as she had rejected the notion of God.

In her autobiography Beauvoir admits that when she was younger she had a marked preference for paintings and statues from which humanity seemed to be absent.[30] Bicycling and hiking in the countryside during the 1930s, she preferred landscapes in which there were no people. Sartre, on the other hand, whom Beauvoir shows as being a step or two ahead of her in this regard, was often indifferent to sites of natural beauty (he was, she says, allergic to chlorophyll) unless they were animated by the presence of people engaged in their daily activities.

Taken prisoner during the war, Marcel is asked by fellow prisoners to paint a fresco on a wall of the prison camp. He complies and is profoundly touched by the appreciation and sincere admiration of the other men in the camp. "That completely upset my ideas,"[31] he remarks. He rejects his former ideas about art and condemns his earlier attempt to create a "painting which could exist all alone, without needing anyone."[32] He embraces the notion of responsibility; presumably he now intends to use his artistic talents in the service of the masses.

Marcel's conversion to social commitment is perhaps even more unconvincing than Jean's acceptance of responsibility for Hélène's abortion. Once again the abstract theme is stated explicitly rather than being incarnated in the characters. Marcel explains his change of heart by saying simply: "In the camp, I understood."[33] The notion of grace would not be inappropriate here, for the acceptance, or awareness, of responsibility, which in turn provides a justification for one's life by making one feel necessary, resembles a Platonic illumination or a stroke of grace that touches a mystic.

Still, the notion of art is singularly ambiguous in *Le Sang des autres*. Marcel's early paintings are described as fine pieces of work created by a robust and original talent. Although they seem to evoke a realm of purity and perfection beyond the human, they exist, as Jean realizes while looking at them, "only because I am here to bestow on them the force of my own life."[34] Beauvoir does not suggest that Marcel's fresco on the camp wall is an artistic success, or even that it is art at all. Artistic criteria are irrelevant in such circumstances. In fact, Beauvoir seems to suggest that they are irrelevant in a world of war, of injustice, of torture.

Later in life Beauvoir would feel increasingly uncomfortable with the very concept of art. It is precisely this later attitude that explains another of her criticisms of *Le Sang des autres*. She came to believe that the novel was too well, or perhaps too artistically composed. In the 1950s (for example, in *Les Mandarins*) she often wrote a deliberately pedestrian prose, believing that such a style (or absence of style) could somehow reflect reality more accurately than the richer, more densely metaphysical prose of her second novel.

Despite Beauvoir's didactic zeal in *Le Sang des autres*, the notions of commitment, of solidarity, of guilt and responsibility are ultimately shown as being as profoundly ambiguous as the notion of art. Jean's commitment to the cause of the working classes reinforces rather than diminishes his spiritual isolation because he realizes that there is an unbridgeable gulf between himself—the bourgeois intellectual who pretends to be a proletarian—and a genuine proletarian. "You choose freely a condition that has been imposed on him,"[35] Marcel tells his friend. Furthermore, the optimism of the explicitly stated messages about fraternity is persistently undermined by Jean's grief at Hélène's bedside—a grief that subtly informs the entire novel, tinging it with loneliness, with sadness, even with despair.

A deeply ironic novel, *Le Sang des autres* is perhaps Beauvoir's most underrated work.

Attracted to the theater by the success of Sartre's *Les Mouches*, 1943 (*The Flies*), and *Huis clos*, 1944

(*No Exit*), Beauvoir spent three months writing her only play, *Les Bouches inutiles* (Useless Mouths), which was produced in November, 1945. It was not a resounding success. When the weather turned cold, the public understandably stayed away from the poorly heated theater. Furthermore, the theater was situated near railroad tracks, and passing trains periodically drowned out the actors' voices. The play closed after some fifty performances.

Dostoevski's eloquent sentence, which had served as the epigraph of *Le Sang des autres*, would have been equally appropriate for *Les Bouches inutiles*. Numerous themes from *Le Sang des autres* are treated, albeit in a somewhat different register, in the play. Once again the basic idea is the inevitability of making choices and the subsequent moral accountability for the choices made.

The action of the play is set in Flanders in the fourteenth century. The inhabitants of the city of Vaucelles have expelled their ruler, the Duke of Burgundy, and have chosen to live in freedom. Now under attack by the Duke, they have been informed that the king of France, an enemy of the Duke's, will come to their rescue in the spring, which is three months hence. However, the city's food supply will last only six more weeks. In desperation the elected city officials decide that in order to save Vaucelles and the principle of freedom they have been fighting for they must round up all the women, children, and old people—in short, all the useless mouths—and force them outside the city gates, where they will surely be killed by the enemy or die of starvation and exposure.

The dramatic interest is focused on the household of the city's chief official, although several scenes show ordinary townspeople swept up in the same terrible

drama. The first of the play's two acts is admirably
conceived and executed. The dialogue is crisp. The
atmosphere is taut and charged with a kind of latent
violence as the city, under seige for weeks, awaits the
council's decision, which is announced at the end of
Act I.

The second act is less satisfactory. Although
caught up in a momentous personal and public crisis,
the characters seem lifeless. Beauvoir's failure here, as
elsewhere in her fictional work, is due to a certain
lack of imaginative intensity. Furthermore, she tends
to reduce the characters to ethical attitudes. Moral
lessons, instead of being worked out imaginatively and
dramatically through the characters, are condensed
into aphorisms that, taken together, constitute a brevi-
ary not only of existentialist thought but of Beauvoir's
curious and ambiguous kind of feminism as well.

In Beauvoir's fictional world, the female characters, who are usually endowed with their creator's
sensibilities, strive essentially for happiness, whereas
her male characters seek to justify their lives by struggling for a cause, by participating in some kind of
oeuvre, either a work of art or a political enterprise.
Curiously, Beauvoir, who in *Le Deuxième Sexe* denies
that there are peculiarly female characteristics, is less
dogmatic in her fiction and joins Colette, whom she
resembles but little, and Rebecca West, to whom she
is somewhat closer, in discerning in women a distinctly
feminine aptitude for happiness, a will-to-live that is
specifically female. However, unlike the characters of
Colette or West, Beauvoir's female characters seem
unable to realize their happiness unless they team up
with a man whose aspirations they espouse and whose
projects they make their own. In other words, her
women cannot get along without men, whereas her
men could, it seems, get along admirably well without

women. One might well ask the question which critic
C. B. Radford posed in the title of an article: "Simone
de Beauvoir: Feminism's Friend or Foe?"[36]

Voicing the wish of most of Beauvoir's heroines,
Catherine in *Les Bouches inutiles* says: "I want to
fashion a life of happiness."[37] And Catherine's husband, speaking with the voice of many of Beauvoir's
male characters, says: "What's at stake is not you or
us, but our community and the future of the whole
world."[38]

At the end of the play the city officials, having
had a change of heart, abandon their plan to expel the
useless mouths. Instead they decide that all citizens
will join hands, and together they will attack the
Burgundian army. They will either die together, or
together they will save their city. Although the conclusion of the play is dramatically unconvincing, it
illustrates the notion of human solidarity and of inter-
human relationships that are not founded on an
awareness of differences between the sexes. "How do
people express love for each other in this world?"
asks one of the female characters. To which Jean-
Pierre, who is portrayed as being in love with her,
answers: "They fight side by side."[39]

Sexual love is valorized in Beauvoir's world only
when it is sublimated into comradeship. Such sublimation usually occurs when the interests of the community are threatened—in moments of social or
political upheaval, in a climate of urgency and crisis.
Love that does not assume the form of a fraternal
struggle against the evils that stalk the world is considered individualistic, a word which for Beauvoir
evokes the bourgeois mentality. It is characterized by
the sorrows of sex. Since only her female characters
are victims of this dolorous kind of love, which is
endured rather than created, it is associated with

woman's subservience—often willingly accepted, Beauvoir admits—in a man-governed world.

Crystallizing during the war years, Beauvoir's
and Sartre's existentialism is essentially a philosophy
of crisis. During the fifties and sixties there were
crises and evils enough in the world to justify Beauvoir's continued cries of outrage. Still, they did not
impinge on her personal life the way World War II
had done, and her postwar indignation, however generous and justified, acquires a more rhetorical, shriller
ring that is less compelling than her earlier attitude.
One might even suspect that her later persistent and
almost hysterical ranting against the injustices that
are all too often built into the social and political
fabric of modern society is in part an attempt to keep
vibrantly alive the notion of comradeship, which transcends the notion of femininity and reduces differences
based on sex to insignificance.

In Beauvoir's fictional world, if a woman is not
a man's comrade in arms, if she does not join him in
a common project (which seldom, if ever, involves
raising a family), she tends to experience love as
abdication of her identity, as servility. In short, virile
comradeship holds sexual love at bay. Françoise in
L'Invitée begins to experience love as suffering only
when she realizes that Pierre views the comradeship
between them differently and less absolutely than she
herself does. At the beginning of *Les Bouches inutiles*,
the aging Catherine declares that if a man and a
woman have both thrown themselves energetically
toward a common future or a common goal, if they
have plunged into the world which their shared will
has fashioned, then they are indissolubly bound to
each other. When she learns that her husband con-
curs with the decision to expel the city's useless
mouths, of which she is one, the bond between them,

which she had for years thought was unbreakable, is severed. Her love turns sour, poisoning the last remaining hours (so she thinks) of her life.

Catherine does not fear death. In fact, she would willingly die in an attempt to save Vaucelles. However, she has been denied the right to choose, and has thus been cast from the community of man, for man, according to existentialist ethics, is characterized by freedom of choice. "I am no longer allowed to make any choices," says Catherine to her husband. "You have deprived me of more than my life."[40] And later in the play she again reproaches him bitterly in terms that recall Hegel's master-slave dialetics: "I am your victim. You are my executioner. We are two strangers."[41]

Young Jean-Pierre also illustrates the play's theme of choice and responsibility. Sent by city officials on the hazardous mission of infiltrating the enemy lines in order to contact the king of France for help, he has returned and is offered a seat on the city council, which he declines. Like Jean Blomart in *Le Sang des autres*, he refuses political activity, for he is unwilling to accept compromise, violence, or responsibility. "I shall keep my hands clean,"[42] he says, not yet realizing that his refusal to sit on the council makes him a tacit accomplice of that body's decision to eliminate the city's useless mouths—a decision Jean-Pierre abhors and for which he soon feels responsible. Had he been on the council he could surely have dissuaded his fellow members from adopting the course of action they ultimately chose.

In his impossible desire to remain pure and guiltless, in his unwillingness to dirty his hands, Jean-Pierre unwittingly becomes "an assassin, an executioner."[43] (Developing a theme similar in some ways to that treated by Beauvoir in *Le Sang des autres* and

Les Bouches inutiles, Sartre entitled one of his most popular—and ironic—plays *Les Mains sales* or *Dirty Hands,* 1948). Again like Jean Blomart, of whom he is essentially a copy, Jean-Pierre learns that risk, danger, and misery are part of human destiny. Why, he asks, should we hope for peace? He succeeds in convincing the council to reverse its decision. As the final curtain falls, the city gate opens. The citizens of Vaucelles, united in a common cause, will meet their fate together before the enemy.

For the Parisian audience of 1945, *Les Bouches inutiles* no doubt had contemporary overtones it would not have for audiences a few years later. Believing that free men can spread freedom to others through the contagion of their heroic example, Beauvoir populated her stage with people who, despite anguished hesitation and an initial false route, eventually choose freedom and solidarity. Although she ultimately failed to breathe life into her characters, the moral seriousness, the earnestness, and persistence with which she confronts ethical and political problems elicit respect and bespeak a mind that does not shun the gravest of issues in this "century of total war."[44]

Begun in 1943, Beauvoir's next novel, *Tous les hommes sont mortels* (*All Men Are Mortal*) was published in 1946. It is an ambitious work, a book in which one can see Beauvoir reaching out for a broad, all-inclusive subject. However, its cargo of ideas is borne aloft by a cast of characters so wooden and unconvincing that the novel never really comes to life, and must in the final analysis be called a relative failure. Still, it marks an important step in Beauvoir's evolution; here she meditates leisurely not only on death and time but also on the history of humanity and on the vanity as well as the validity of political action. Beauvoir later described the book accurately when she called it "an organized digression whose themes are not theses but points of departure toward unpredictable meanderings."[45]

As the novel opens, Régine, a young and ambitious actress, is taking a final curtain call. The first sentence is interesting for a number of reasons:

The curtain went up again. Régine bowed and smiled. Under the light of the large chandelier, pink spots flickered on the multicolored dresses and dark suits. In every face there were eyes, and reflected in every pair of eyes was Régine, bowing and smiling. The roar of cataracts, the rumbling of avalanches filled the old theater. An impetuous force tore her from the earth and thrust her toward heaven.[46]

This sentence bears a distinct resemblance to other opening sentences in Beauvoir's novels: "Françoise looked up" (*L'Invitée*); "When he opened the door, all eyes turned toward him" (*Le Sang des autres*); "Henri cast a final glance at the sky" (*Les Mandarins*). Sight is the primary sense in Beauvoir's world. In her autobiography she declares that she can conceive of living without any one of the senses except sight. Her fundamental enterprise is to *see* reality, to unmask the truth (*dévoiler* is one of her favorite words), and then to expose it to the eyes of others.

Eager to demystify and to strip away from reality the veneer we conveniently (and often for our profit) lay over it, Beauvoir returns repeatedly to notions of pretence and façade. In her early works she is concerned mainly with self-deception; in her later books she tends to associate hypocrisy and deceit with the bourgeoisie, whose traditional values are usually seen as frauds. Beauvoir's preoccupation with delusion and sham explains one of the most striking features of her style—the persistent use of theatrical terminology. Words such as drama, role, act, farce, tragedy, comedy, etc., appear frequently in her work. (Incidentally, the opening sentence of *La Femme rompue* is: "The décor is extraordinary.")

Closely associated with Beauvoir's concern for appearances and her use of a vocabulary that suggests the theater is her frequent mention of mirrors. A rich symbol, the mirror is often used in her work to suggest not only narcissism but also a character's search for his own identity. Significantly, it is Beauvoir's heroines rather than her heroes who peer into a mirror in a vain attempt to define themselves and to give meaning to their lives. " 'My eyes, my face,' thought Hélène somewhat excitedly. 'Me. Nobody else in the world is me' "[47] (*Le Sang des autres*). From the existentialist perspective, meaning can come only from acts, from a project, and the fact that so many of Beauvoir's heroines identify with the image of themselves that is reflected in a mirror, in the eyes of a lover or, as in the case of Régine, in the eyes of an applauding public, is a comment on the inauthenticity and passivity that is their lot.

Narcissistic posturing before a mirror suggests a solipsistic attitude, an entrapment in the circle of self, a denial of transcendence toward the future or of intentionality, to use the word existentialists borrowed from Husserl. It thus suggests a rejection of life itself. Indeed, in Beauvoir's work, especially in *Tous les hommes sont mortels*, reflections in mirrors, in eyes, or in water often evoke the presence of emptiness or of death.

But mirrors, like the eyes of others, may also reflect an objective image which the subject is forced to recognize as a true image of himself and from which he cannot flee. Beauvoir looked into her mirror when she reached the age of forty and saw old age: "Forty. Forty-one. Old age was lying in wait. From the depths of the mirror, it was on the look-out for me."[48] Mirrors, like the gaze of others, like the judgment of our own moral conscience, may thus reveal to us an implacable truth about ourselves. *

In the character of Régine, Beauvoir has again created a young heroine whose principal problem is precisely the one the author identified as her own: a reluctance to accept the fact that others exist as autonomously as she. Constantly irritated by the very existence of others, Régine dislikes going to sleep because she realizes that while she sleeps others will still be awake and that she will have no power over them. When she was an adolescent she rejected God because He loved others as well as herself. "I don't want to be a blade of grass,"[49] she says several times in the novel.

She is cut from the same cloth as other of Beauvoir's young women, notably Xavière, Hélène, Clarice (*Les Bouches inutiles*) and Nadine (*Les Mandarins*). Egotistical, surly, defiant, and ill-mannered, she bristles with rage whenever she feels that her freedom is somehow being limited. Hers is an attitude of continual revolt against traditional values, but more especially against the limitations that result from her own character, from her own nature as a mortal being. Closed upon themselves, the young women who populate Beauvoir's fiction no doubt represent a revolt against all those forces, societal or biological, which tend to push them into preordained roles in life. However, viewed not as incarnations of an idea but as fictional characters endowed with a psychological makeup, they are narrow-minded, petulant, and singularly unpleasant. Beauvoir has repeatedly displayed her considerable talent for creating disagreeable young heroines.

Régine cannot tolerate the sight of happy people. "When people are alive, when I see them in love and happy," she muses, "I feel as if I were being assassinated."[50] "I don't like to see other people happy, and I enjoy making them feel my power."[51] This decidedly unpleasant character trait crops up in so many of Beauvoir's heroines that one is not surprised to find more than a few traces of it in the author's portrait of herself. It is tempting to speculate (although this sort of thing can easily be overdone) that Beauvoir's hatred of the bourgeoisie as well as her generally hostile attitude toward marriage and maternity are rooted in a reluctance to accept as genuine any form of happiness that is different from her own. In *La Vieillesse*, 1970 (*The Coming of Age*) she nearly says as much when she defines and then rejects contemptuously a certain kind of happiness which she chooses to call bourgeois: "One of the major preoccupations of a bourgeois is to guarantee his own happiness. He thinks he can obtain it through virtue, through easy mediocrity, by cultivating family ties and bonds of friendship. Essentially, happiness is conceived as repose."[52] Happiness, Beauvoir insists, is not to be found in ataraxia, or a state of total tranquillity, but rather in an intensification, a heightening of life.

If ataraxia is a denial of life, so too is Régine's desperate desire to reside in a superior realm (evoked in the novel's first sentence by the word "heaven"), there to be transfixed in singular and immutable glory. Like other of Beauvoir's heroines, Régine thinks of herself as unique and is tormented by the thought that every other individual thinks of himself in the same way, thus denying her a privileged position in the world. Beauvoir, who in *Mémoires d'une jeune fille rangée* insists on her own youthful desire to be unique, announces repeatedly in later books, perhaps with a bit too much emphasis to be completely believed, that she has finally lost that particular dream of girlhood. As late as 1972 she wrote once again: "At last I have lost the puerile illusion of being situated in the exact center of the universe."[53]

Régine has not lost that illusion and, refusing to accept the contingencies of existence, aspires toward the plenitude and unalterability of absolute being. When she meets Fosca and learns that he is immortal, she falls in love with him, believing that once enshrined in the heart of an immortal, she too will gain some measure of immortality.[54]

It does not work out as she had hoped. As Fosca relates the incredible story of his life, which has already spanned several centuries (his story constitutes the main body of the novel), Régine gradually realizes that from the perspective of eternity any single life is so ephemeral that it is reduced to insignificance.

Count Fosca was born in 1279 in the Italian city-state of Carmona.[55] Eager to make Carmona one of the principal cities in Italy, he threw himself impetuously into the murky waters of political intrigue, struggling always to acquire ever greater power and to expand his city's influence. He strove toward a definite, finite goal, and lived passionately and intensely.

When Carmona was attacked and nearly conquered by the Genoese, Fosca drank an elixir that made him immortal, thinking that by becoming invulnerable he could save his city and complete the tasks he had wished to accomplish. This he did, only to discover that an empty eternity stretched out before him. At first he set other goals for himself, hoping to recapture his zest for life and the sense of urgency

that had made life vibrant and meaningful. As time
went by, however, he gradually ceased to share other
men's hopes, their fears, anguish, or joy. From his
perspective as an immortal, human activities seemed
to be an endless repetition, generation after generation, of the same futile gestures.

Beauvoir constructs Fosca's long account of his
life in a series of large historical frescoes, rich in detail
and full of figures that are engaged in strife and violent activities, mostly war and conquest. In the six-
teenth century, Fosca became the principal counselor
of Charles V (known also as Charles I of Spain) and
tried to assure peace and the good of humanity by
working for the effective re-establishment of the Holy
Roman Empire with Charles as its ruler. The irony,
of course, is that one cannot create happiness for
others. Nor can one determine for others what their
good is. Furthermore, it is not even happiness that
people desire; they want to feel that they are alive.
As one of the characters tells Fosca: "I must be able
to feel myself alive—even if it causes my death."[56]

In the seventeenth century, Fosca roamed through
the New World. During much of the eighteenth century, he frequented aristocratic Parisian salons. Up to
this point Beauvoir's general view of human history
is resolutely pessimistic. It is seen as an old refrain
that is repeated over and over. However, for each
individual person, uniquely situated in a precise time
and place, it appears fresh and as yet undetermined.
The individual freely fixes his goals and struggles
toward them. For him, the present moment acquires
meaning only to the extent that it is projected toward
the future. The principal dimension of time in Beauvoir's work is a present that is penetrated with intimations of the future. As an immortal, Fosca is outside of time, outside of life. In this context, death is

our greatest blessing (an argument unlikely to convince many readers), for without it there would be no time, no thrust toward the future, which is the very essence of life. Furthermore, since the present is perceived only as flight from, as motion toward, it cannot be lived for itself. As Sartre put it in *L'Être et le néant*: "The present does not exist. It can be perceived only as something that vanishes."[57]

In the remarkable pages devoted to a discussion of "the instant" in *Pyrrhus et Cinéas*, Beauvoir analyzes the fallacy of hedonism: pleasure, if it remains steady and unchanging, is no longer sensed as pleasure, but as the absence of pleasure, as boredom. "I can feel pleasure," she observes, "only when I get out of myself, and when the object that is the source of my enjoyment becomes a means whereby I can engage my being in the world."[58]

In Beauvoir's vast frescoes of life since the thirteenth century, people (mostly men, since she always shows men as the controllers of society) throw themselves audaciously into the tumult of life. Restless, active, purposeful beings, they move ceaselessly from place to place, always killing, building, and then tearing down. In Beauvoir's world, effort, discipline and will power are supreme qualities; grace, insouciance, charm, and finesse are valued but little.

When her fictional characters attain the specific goal for which they were striving, they jubilantly celebrate their victory. A *fête* (a key word in Beauvoir's vocabulary) is that exceptional and perfect moment in which the instant, or the present, seems to be seized and savored for itself. It is a communal celebration that has meaning only in relationship to the past, for it is the culmination of an enterprise that has finally been realized. "Joy is not a separation from the world; it presupposes my existence in the world;

it presupposes my past."[59] The consciousness, radiant with triumph and joy, conceives the *fête* as a temporary halt in time. Of course, the *fête* itself soon falls into the past, into history. The victory it celebrates becomes the point of departure for a new project which, if it too is realized, will eventually culminate in similar festivities.

All of Beauvoir's novels, but especially *Tous les hommes sont mortels,* are punctuated with joyous celebrations. Her autobiography, too, is marked by *fêtes* commemorating victories both small and great. The most elaborately described and intensely felt *fête* in her work is the liberation of Paris in 1944, recounted both in the autobiography and in *Les Mandarins.*

Fosca cannot participate in man's celebrations for, from his perspective, human triumphs are pathetically ephemeral. "Behind all the words, the gestures, the smiles, lurked the fundamental deceit, the emptiness."[60] The riches men amass, the objects with which they surround themselves, point to the meaninglessness and vanity of human enterprises *sub specie aeternitatis.* Beauvoir's immense frescoes of mankind's accomplishments, which are materialized in the form of wealth, of palaces, of expanding empires, curiously resemble vast still lifes. A pictorial representation of the things of this world, a still life was traditionally called a *vanitas.* Mastery of illusionistic technique permitted a painter to create an image of worldly riches which, for all their immediacy, remained illusory. A still life, a picture of things, a *vanitas,* was considered for centuries to be essentially an artifact designed to bear witness to the transcience of mortality, a reminder of the vanity of which the Biblical Preacher spoke. In fact, there is a preacher in *Tous les hommes sont mortels* who echoes *Ecclesiastes* when he says: "Wordly riches are nothing but vanity."[61]

If Fosca's indifference and inability to experience human passions and desires illustrate the vanity of human activity *sub specie aeternitatis,* Beauvoir's portrayal of history as an endless repetition of doomed hopes points to the vanity of man's endeavors *sub specie historiae.* Indeed, *Tous les hommes sont mortels* implicitly rejects as useless the notion not only of eternity but of history as well, that is to say history as an academic discipline practiced by professional historians. Beauvoir condemns the view, so solidly embodied in the work of German thinkers from Hegel to Spengler, that history is an expression of destiny. Denying determinism of any kind and exalting freedom, she categorically rejects the notion of causality, one of the presuppositions of historical research. The past is dead and can in no way bind us; it cannot limit our freedom of choice.

The pessimism of Beauvoir's picture of earlier centuries is somewhat attenuated in her evocation of the nineteenth and twentieth centuries. Fosca joins workers who struggle against the political, social, and economic oppression that resulted from the industrial revolution. Although in his eyes the activities of his nineteenth- and twentieth-century contemporaries are as vain as those of previous generations, in the eyes of Beauvoir herself there is a difference, for the battles fought by Fosca's proletarian friends are essentially the battles she was soon going to fight. The struggle to improve the often desperate lot of workers and to establish a socialist state belonged to Beauvoir's future and not to the past. Certain accomplishments, such as the abolition of child labor laws and the improvement of working conditions, are not seen as futile activities but as real achievements leading to still greater progress in the future.

Written during the war, *Tous les hommes sont mortels* contains intimations of Beauvoir's postwar

social and political commitment. Toward the end of
the novel, Armand, one of Fosca's friends, tells him
that a man must live in the present, that he must strive
to extend as much as possible his hold on the future.
"A limited future; a limited life," he continues. "That
is our lot as men. If I knew that in fifty years it would
be against the law to use children in factories, against
the law to make men work more than ten hours a
day, if I knew that people would choose their own
representatives, that the press would be free, then I
would be satisfied."[62] Beauvoir will soon have the
same attitude as Armand toward the future. She will
never quite forget, however, that viewed from a Fosca-
like distance this very attitude must be judged vain
and futile.

Rejecting the bourgeois individualism which she
later saw as the principal characteristic of her prewar
mentality, suspicious of all her former values—even
generosity and authenticity—because they seemed to
be rooted in individualistic concerns and did not take
into account the existence of the masses, Beauvoir
was soon to embrace Marxism as the political ideology
most likely to bring about a socialist state and to improve the lot of mankind. Passionately intent on coming to grips with the realities of the present and on
molding the future to the extent that she was able,
she threw herself more fervently than ever into the
welter of life. She would soon conclude her "moral
phase" with the publication of two slender volumes
of essays, and then, with eager anticipation, leave for
a four-month visit to the United States, the country
which, in 1946, seemed to her to incarnate the future.

Among the first books published in France after
the war were *Pyrrhus et Cinéas* and *Le Sang des autres*.
Having endured some four years of German occupa-

tion, France was eager, Beauvoir says, to express its vitality by asserting its leadership in two areas for which it had been internationally famous: fashion and literature. Sartre's reputation, which before the war had been based largely on his success as a novelist, had grown with the highly successful productions of his first plays. His massive philosophical treatise, *L'Être et le néant,* which when published in 1943 had not aroused a great deal of interest, was soon to be the source of endless polemics.

As Sartre's companion and associate, Beauvoir shared in his fame. When journalists dubbed her "Notre-Dame de Sartre" or "La Grande Sartreuse," she laughed along with everyone else and continued to construct her own literary work whose philosophical substructure, she recognized, rests to a large extent on Sartre's thought ("it is through him that problems have presented themselves to me"[63]), but whose qualities and distinctive characteristics are very much her own.

In January, 1945, Sartre visited the United States with a group of French journalists. Beauvoir, too, soon had a chance to travel. Her brother-in-law, who was director of the French Institute in Lisbon, invited her to give a series of lectures in Portugal. On February 28, 1945 she arrived in Lisbon, overwhelmed first by the luxury of the shops which, after the dearth of merchandise in French stores, seemed staggering to her, and secondly, by the oppressive nature of the Salazar regime and the appalling poverty of a large percentage of the Portuguese people.

In the fall of the same year appeared the first issue of the periodical *Les Temps modernes (Modern Times),* of which Sartre was the director (for a time he shared the directorship with the leading French phenomenologist, Merleau-Ponty). Beauvoir wrote ar-

ticles for the new journal, which rapidly became one
of the most important in France, and shared editorial
responsibilities.

Those were intensely busy months for Beauvoir.
Her circle of acquaintances expanded so quickly that
she soon felt as if she knew all the important writers,
artists, cineastes, and journalists who were eagerly
striving to make their mark in the new France that
was emerging from the ashes of war. With a touch of
nostalgia for the virile comradeship of those active
days and with just a hint of cozy complacency, Beauvoir later wrote that in the three or four years following the war, whenever she opened the newspaper she
felt as if she were opening her own mail, so familiar
was she with the people who made the news or who
wrote about it.

Early in 1945 Beauvoir had toyed with the idea
of elaborating on some of the ethical positions and
certain of the problems of social morality which she
felt were implicit in *L'Être et le néant*, but which
Sartre had left undeveloped and unresolved, announc-
ing at the end of his bulky treatise that he intended
to treat them more fully "in a coming work"—a work
he has never written. When Camus, who was an
editor at the publishing house of Gallimard, asked
her to write an essay on ethics for a series of books
he was promoting, she agreed. The result was *Pour
une morale de l'ambiguïté*, published in 1947, and
immediately translated into English under the title of
The Ethics of Ambiguity (1948).

In 1948 Beauvoir's *Existentialisme et la sagesse
des nations* (*Existentialism and the Wisdom of Nations*), a collection of four essays that had appeared
previously in *Les Temps modernes*, was also published. Her phrase "the wisdom of nations" is an
ironic reference to those shopworn clichés that usually

pass for moral wisdom in our culture. Less substantial than *Pour une morale de l'ambiguïté, Existentialisme et la sagesse des nations* is essentially a volume of occasional pieces.

Pour une morale de l'ambiguïté is a kind of handbook of existentialist ethics. Many of the notions Beauvoir here deals with—time, *fêtes*, action, the existence of others—were treated in fictional form in *Tous les hommes sont mortels.*

Beauvoir begins by picking up Sartre's argument, presented near the end of *L'Être et le néant,* that man's basic wish is to fuse his freedom with the impermeability of things, to achieve a state of being in which the *en-soi* (being-in-itself) and the *pour-soi* (being-for-itself) are synthesized. If one abandons for a moment the existentialist jargon that gives a distinctive cachet to the argument but that perhaps muddies the water more than is necessary, this simply means that man is a conscious being surrounded by objects, and that he cannot lose himself in them, he cannot obliterate the difference between himself and things outside himself. Such a fusion, Sartre states, can be called God. "Man," he continues, "is the being who wants to be God"—a contradictory ideal, for to be God, or to be immortal, would be to deny one's mortal existence, as is illustrated by Fosca in *Tous les hommes sont mortels.*

Man's ambiguity resides precisely in the fact that he strives toward this ideal, toward an absolute, and never attains anything but a relative state. Unlike thinkers of Neoplatonic or idealistic bent who attempt to conceal this essential ambiguity by positing a guarantor, some kind of absolute being or Idea that is outside man but that envelops him, assimilates him, and secretly assures him of divine solicitude, Beauvoir insists that man must not try to eliminate the ambiguity and inherent tension of his situation because it is precisely they which characterize his existence. Nothing is more antithetical to her thought than the assertion by the great German poet Novalis that "perhaps the loftiest task of the loftiest spirit is to destroy the principle of contradiction."[64]

Since a relative state is the only one an individual can know, it paradoxically becomes for him an absolute, his absolute. In one of those densely compact, crystalline, and teasing sentences that French writers often favor when they wish to express the very quintessence of their thought, Beauvoir writes: "Man is a being whose being is non-being."[65] Or, expressed differently: "Man fulfills himself in the heart of ephemerality, or not at all."[66]

This view has decidedly tragic overtones. But it is not unremittingly pessimistic. Man's ambiguity is such that Fosca's pessimism, or rather his indifference, and Armand's optimism are both right. One of Beauvoir's intents in *Pour une morale de l'ambiguïté* is to reaffirm the element of failure and the presence of death in every human existence. She here distinguishes her attitude from that of Communists who, she says, are not interested in man as an individual, but only as a member of a class, of a collectivity. Once again, but in a different register, Beauvoir is concerned with the relationship between the self and others, with the problems created by the apparent contradiction between the radically individualistic perspective implied in the notion of man's freedom, and, on the other hand, man's need to live in a society.

The basic philosophical problem in existentialist ethics is in reconciling the view that we can and should choose to be free and autonomous beings with the equally important view that we are in some essential way responsible to others. To say that we choose to be responsible is begging the question, for if my responsibility is necessary and unavoidable, as Beauvoir seems to hold, my freedom of choice would appear to be limited. Beauvoir does not really face this problem squarely. She simply suggests that the fact that we are autonomous beings somehow places us under an obligation to respect the moral freedom of others, an argument which is less than completely satisfactory.

Indeed, *Pour une morale de l'ambiguïté* is much closer to an existentialist declaration of faith than to a work of philosophy. Short on analyses but rich in maxims that are trenchant, provocative, and eminently quotable, it is close in tone to the works of seventeenth- and eighteenth-century French moralists, and thus approaches one of the grandest and most venerable traditions in French literature.

In fact, a long section of *Pour une morale de l'ambiguïté* curiously resembles one of the most famous works of that rich tradition, La Bruyère's *Les Caractères* or *Characters* (1688), whose gallery of human types is among the most familiar passages in French literature. With an incisive pen, Beauvoir, too, sketches portraits of types: the serious man, the nihilist, the adventurer, the passionate man. She later grew to dislike *Pour une morale de l'ambiguïté*, saying that of all her books this one annoyed her the most. The reasons are easy to see. In describing types she had succumbed to the tendency to idealize, to present ideal forms as if they had a reality outside of any precise social situation. She later maintained that to attempt to define ethical stances and moral attitudes without defining the peculiar situations that give them their unique coloration is to create portraits that are arbitrary and abstract, and ultimately false to reality.

One other topic discussed in *Pour une morale de l'ambiguïté* is worthy of special note. Beauvoir firmly links the notion of art to that of *fêtes*. From Beauvoir's atheistic perspective, existence is a relentless motion (*échappement* is her word, which suggests leakage or escape, as of gas) toward nothingness. Societies, she says, instituted *fêtes* for the purpose of affirming existence in the present, of stopping momentarily the movement toward transcendence. As well as being an exaltation of the present, a *fête* is also a communion with others. However, since we can never possess the present, this joy and communion cannot be prolonged beyond the duration of the *fête*, and we are left with a feeling of fatigue, emptiness, and disappointment.

Alluding to the Dionysian origin of the theater, Beauvoir points out that music, dance, and poetry have traditionally been associated with the *fête*. One of the roles of art, she explains, is to give a durable form to the passionate affirmation of existence that is expressed in *fêtes*. Indeed, art for her is essentially a *fête* that does not end. Her view of art is diametrically opposed to that expressed in the phrase "art for art's sake." She condemns the *nouveau roman* mainly because it is devoid of ethical content and because it is utterly joyless, that is to say, lifeless.

The great value Beauvoir attaches to joy is important and should be emphasized. "The idea of liberation can have a concrete meaning only if the joy of living is affirmed in each one of us at every moment. The movement toward freedom assumes its real, its physical form in the world by being channeled into pleasure, into happiness."[67] Although her work as a whole is grave, even weighty (and who would deny that a work intended to reveal the political and social realities of the years 1940-70 could be anything else), it is profoundly marked with Beauvoir's ardent desire to live honestly and passionately, and to express not only the horror but also the joy of existence.

4

No Time

for Boredom

Beauvoir alludes approvingly to the Biblical condemnation of those who are "lukewarm, neither cold nor hot."[1] Indeed, she belongs to the race of the energetic, even the violent. In 1972 she looked back on her life and saw in her childish tantrums, in her lust to live and to write, in her impatience, her occasional fits of despair, her intense dislikes, her dogmatism, and in her immense creative activity an expression of one of the principal traits of her character—a trait which she defines as an urgent need to pursue her desires, her refusals, her acts, and her thoughts to their conclusion. Writing was one mode through which she expressed her feverish will to live. "Writing," she noted, "is not a matter of recording what one knows, but of prolonging an experience."[2]

Few pages in her work convey as vividly as do the opening pages of *L'Amérique au jour le jour*, 1948 (*America Day by Day*) Beauvoir's appetite for experience, her sense of adventure, of joyful conquest curiously coupled with an equally strong desire to be conquered, to be surprised, overwhelmed, swept off her feet, indeed, ravished by unexpected, novel, and extraordinary events.

L'Amérique au jour le jour chronicles Beauvoir's four-month visit to the United States. It is presented in diary form, the first entry being the date of her arrival in New York, January 25, 1947, and the last, the day of her departure, May 20. Although she lectured at various colleges during her stay, her time was largely her own. She admits in the preface that there were important aspects of American life and culture she did not see: she visited no factories, had no contact with workers, spoke with no important political figures. The book is presented, not as a sociological study (although many pages would fall into this category), but as an account of how "America was revealed to a particular consciousness: my own."[3]

Published in the United States in 1953, *L'Amérique au jour le jour* was widely misunderstood. The hysteria of the McCarthy era was such that any book on the United States by a French author who sympathized with Communist Russia was bound to be labeled anti-American. And then, Beauvoir was indeed critical of certain aspects of American life: racism, conformism, a puritan morality that convinced Americans it was their God-given duty to impose their will on other peoples, a refusal to face up to the reality of evil and human suffering, and, most distressing of all, a sense of helplessness and resignation among the young who, because they felt unable to change their world, to mold their future, seemed listless and submissive. The latter observation was perceptive and helps explain the enormous impact of existentialism on American college students in the 1950s and 1960s. With its espousal of action, freedom and responsibility, existentialism was for many American youths a heady and, on the whole, beneficial tonic.

Beauvoir's criticisms of the United States pale in comparison with the almost masochistically critical books many Americans wrote about their country in the 1960s. In fact, the harshest criticism in her book is directed against the French who live in America and who, she says, "with only a very few exceptions incarnate all the faults of their country and embody only very fleetingly its qualities."[4]

Genuinely interested in the United States whose language she spoke fluently (if with a heavy accent), whose literature and history she knew, whose jazz she had long been fond of, Beauvoir discovered a country much more real, much more complex than the legendary land she had imagined. Incomplete, as books of this kind necessarily are, and occasionally inaccurate,

L'Amérique au jour le jour is often a remarkably perceptive book, written by a lucid, and on the whole, understanding observer.

Beauvoir spent six months in 1948 writing *L'Amérique au jour le jour*. "I couldn't decide to put America behind me," she noted in the third volume of her autobiography, *La Force des choses*; "I tried to prolong my trip by writing a book."[5] If she had difficulty in detaching herself from America it was essentially because, while in Chicago, she had begun a liaison with the American novelist Nelson Algren. In *L'Amérique au jour le jour*, Beauvoir does not name the Americans she met, but identifies them simply by their initials. She mentions N. A., who was her host in Chicago, but in no way reveals their personal relationship. Several years later, after the break-up of their sporadic, transatlantic liaison, which was marked by numerous crises and abundant tears as well as by happiness, Beauvoir recounted her affair with Algren first in fictionalized form in *Les Mandarins* and then in *La Force des choses*.

The initial pact between Beauvoir and Sartre contained a provision for "contingent love affairs."[6] So touchy was Beauvoir about any infringement of her freedom that in her view fidelity was necessarily incompatible with freedom. "Can there be any possible reconciliation between fidelity and freedom?" she asks in her autobiography. That millions of people might honestly answer "yes" does not occur to her. As usual, Beauvoir does not for a moment entertain the notion that any rational human being could hold a view different from her own. She continues in the peremptory tone that annoys numerous readers: "Often preached, rarely practiced, complete fidelity is usually experienced by those who impose it upon themselves as a mutilation; they console themselves for it by sublimation or by drink."[7]

Beauvoir's views on the couple, on fidelity, on the second sex, and old age are at times too personally oriented to be completely valid. Too often she looks in her mirror and thinks she sees humanity. However, it must also be said that in defending her freedom and her right to "contingent love affairs" she was demanding for women privileges which, she felt, had been reserved for men.

Beauvoir seems to have sensed from the beginning of her relationship with Sartre that she could count on him to be faithless. Indeed, Sartre took advantage of the proviso permitting a certain amount of amorous straying. Perhaps the most serious of such affairs was the liaison he had begun with an American woman, identified as M., during his visit to the United States early in 1945. Infatuated with M., he had returned to New York to visit her in December of that year. During the next several years, the relationship between Beauvoir and Sartre was put to several rather severe tests but was never really in jeopardy. The intruder was always eventually expelled. "We maintained throughout all deviations from the main path a 'certain fidelity,' "[8] Beauvoir later declared with the satisfaction of a *petite bourgeoise* who, despite everything, has managed to keep up a façade of respectability. Despite the occasional distress, their "contingent love affairs" were ultimately seen as enriching experiences.

Shortly after Beauvoir's return to France in May, 1947, M. settled down in Paris, intending to stay. Beauvoir and Sartre moved from the city to a small hotel on the edge of Paris, and Sartre went in to Paris on certain evenings to see M. Beauvoir affirms that she was perfectly satisfied with this arrangement. However, M., who persisted in holding the antediluvian view that fidelity was somehow related to love, was not satisfied. It was in this atmosphere of considerable tension that Beauvoir prolonged her American visit by writing *L'Amérique au jour le jour*.

In September she returned to Chicago, exploring the city (with Algren as guide) much more thoroughly than she had done on her first visit a few months earlier. The impressions of both visits were combined into one composite picture of Chicago in *L'Amérique au jour le jour*. Algren asked her to stay in America, but she knew that she could not permanently live and work in the United States any more than he could live and work in Paris.

The next two years were particularly busy ones for Beauvoir. In February, 1948, she accompanied Sartre to Berlin. Then in the spring she returned to the United States for a two-month stay with Algren. They boarded a boat in Cincinnati and traveled down the Mississippi to New Orleans. From there they went on to Guatemala and Mexico. In June, 1949, Algren visited Paris. The two of them traveled to Italy and North Africa. In the summer of 1950 Beauvoir was back in the United States, spending most of her two-month stay at Algren's recently acquired cottage on Lake Michigan. She went back to France and then returned to Chicago in October.

Algren had become increasingly uneasy about being so emotionally attached to a woman who was not able, or willing, to stay with him more than a few weeks each year. He had begun talking about remarrying his ex-wife. When Beauvoir said goodby to him at the end of October she knew it was for good. She had an overnight stop in New York before catching the plane for Paris. Recounting her departure from Chicago, she wrote: "In the taxi, the train, the plane, and during the evening in New York as I watched a film by Walt Disney in which animals endlessly devoured each other, I wept without stopping."[9]

As full of travel as those years were (and Beauvoir also visited Africa twice with Sartre during the same period), they were also full of work. Vacationing for her, she once explained, usually meant working somewhere else. Indeed, she never separated living from writing. "My desire to learn about the world is intimately tied up with my desire to express my experience,"[10] she said in a revealing sentence.

As early as 1946 Beauvoir had toyed with the idea of writing directly about herself. Impressed with her friend Michel Leiris's fine autobiographical volume *L'Âge d'homme*, she too wished to write "sacrificial essays in which the author strips himself bare without excuses."[11] She started to take notes and then discussed the project with Sartre, who suggested that she first examine the extent to which being a woman had colored her existence. Thinking about the issue raised by Sartre, Beauvoir was astonished to realize that the world was masculine, that she had been brought up on myths which had been forged by men and that her reactions to situations had been totally different from those of a boy. Setting aside for the time being her plan to write a "personal confession," she decided to study the status of women, and went to the National Library where she began amassing the data and statistics that were to go into her book.

Completed in 1949, the work was published in two stout volumes totaling more than one thousand pages. Finding an appropriate title had been something of a problem. At first Beauvoir had thought about *L'Autre* (The Other One) or even *La Seconde* (The Second One); the latter had the disadvantage of having already been used by Colette for the title of a novel. Discussing the matter with Sartre and their friend Jacques Bost, Beauvoir suggested *L'Autre Sexe* (The Other Sex). Bost countered with *Le Deu-*

xième Sexe (The Second Sex) and, after thinking it over, they decided that this was the most suitable title. The work is in fact dedicated to Bost. (One might have thought that Beauvoir would have dedicated this book, of all her books, to a woman. But by and large she seems to have been more comfortable in the society of men than of women.)

It is certainly not without significance that Beauvoir came upon the subject of her book "almost by accident,"[12] as she puts it, while seeking a literary form that would permit her to talk about herself. As a study of womankind, *Le Deuxième Sexe* clearly belongs to anthropological sociology. But while analyzing the situation of women in general, Beauvoir was preparing the way for a study of a particular woman—herself. Seen in this light *Le Deuxième Sexe* is a long preamble to the four volumes of the autobiography she would later write. Interestingly, the last of the four volumes, *Tout compte fait* (*All Said and Done*), a book in which Beauvoir meditates on her old age, was preceded by another weighty sociological study, *La Vieillesse* (*The Coming of Age*). Here too the general study is followed by an examination of her own particular case.

In both *Le Deuxième Sexe* and *La Vieillesse* Beauvoir deals with themes that are central to all her fiction and thought. Her method in both books is similar. In each case she states widely accepted facts —the hostility and discrimination women too often encounter when they move out of the home into a larger, male-dominated arena and the psychological and economic distress, often anguish, that frequently accompanies old age. She then attributes blame to suit her own philosophical and ideological views.

Beauvoir suggests few practical solutions to the problems she raises. Like all her books—whether novels, essays, travel books, or autobiographical volumes—her sociological studies are designed to reveal a truth. As critic C. B. Radford has pointed out, each of Beauvoir's books is an account of an education. In the novels it is the fictional characters who gradually perceive reality; in her nonfiction it is Beauvoir herself who writes her books to mark the various stages on her way toward truth.

Le Deuxième Sexe is a mammoth edifice that rests on two slender postulates: first, that man, conceiving of himself as the essential being, the subject, has made woman into the unessential being, the object, the Other; second, that there is no such thing as feminine nature and that all notions of femininity are therefore artificial. Both postulates are enunciated in the introduction and are derived from concepts elaborated by Sartre in *L'Être et le néant,* a book to which Beauvoir frequently refers as if to a sacred text whose validity and authority no right thinking person could question. "The perspective I am adopting," she announces at the end of the introduction, "is that of existentialist ethics."[13]

Borrowing directly from Sartre, Beauvoir declares that the category of otherness is inherent in consciousness itself. "Otherness is a fundamental category of human thought. No group ever conceives of itself as the One without immediately setting up the Other in opposition to itself."[14] Furthermore, awareness of otherness arouses a feeling of hostility. The dialectics of aggression is one of the most characteristic features of Beauvoir's work. Not for a moment does she imagine that opposites can sustain and complement each other. In order to assert itself, each consciousness must strive for the destruction, the annihilation of the other. This, in fact, was the theme of *L'Invitée,* written before existentialism had yet been codified into a philosophical or ideological doctrine.

Given her basic view of the aggressivity of the

consciousness, its intolerance of anything different
from itself, its cliquishness, the question is not why
men might be hostile toward women (they are also
hostile toward men), but why men, at another level
of awareness, have defined themselves as the essential
ingredient in humanity, relegating women to the an-
cillary role of otherness. "Although women are not
the only Others," Beauvoir states, "the fact remains
that women are invariably defined as Others."[15]

For women, it is of course men who constitute
the Others. The important point, however, is that
women, for reasons Beauvoir will analyze in her study,
have accepted the male point of view and have conceived of themselves as unessential. They have by and
large consented to be either an object or, to the extent
that they incarnate certain of man's dreams, an image.
In either case they exist for men and not for themselves.

Beauvoir's second postulate—that there is no
feminine nature—is derived from one of the most
fundamental of existentialist principles, namely that
there is no human nature, the word nature being
understood here as essence. Sartre expressed this notion in his famous formula, existence precedes essence,
by which he meant basically that man need not conform to any archetype, that only in the very process
of living does he create his own values, his being, his
essence. If there is no archetypal human nature, there
obviously can be no feminine or masculine nature. As
Beauvoir expresses it in one of the most telling aphorisms in *Le Deuxième Sexe*: "One is not born a
woman; rather one becomes a woman."[16]

Still, there are biological differences between men
and women, and Beauvoir, armed with these two
existentialist notions, begins her study by examining
woman's biological makeup. The heart of the first

chapter is a long (five- or six-page) description of the menstrual cycle. Beauvoir details the entire process: the bursting of the Graafian follicle, the egg's descent down the Fallopian tube, the various chemical changes in the body, the pain, the bleeding. The most striking feature of her description is the emotional coloration of the vocabulary, which is rich in words suggesting viscosity, oozing, slipping, loss, loathing. Later, in her autobiography, Beauvoir will recall in similar terms her own menstrual difficulties during adolescence.

The main reason for her disgust, however, is not any personal reaction to menstruation; it is recognition of the fact that a woman is forced to submit to menstruation whether she wills it or not. Beauvoir tends to view the whole childbearing process as serving the species to the detriment of the individual woman.

Although Beauvoir and Sartre insist on one's absolute freedom of choice, they of course recognize that certain given factors affect that choice. These factors constitute what Sartre calls one's situation. The degree to which an individual is distinctly human is measured by the extent to which he transcends his particular situation. A woman's situation is naturally determined in part by the biological factors associated with menstruation and childbearing. She can only become human by transcending, which usually means reacting against, these factors. The logic of Beauvoir's argument leads her to affirm that "humanity is not an animal species"[17] and that a woman becomes human to the extent that she reacts against her nature, the word nature here meaning those biological factors that help determine her situation.

Beauvoir modifies this extreme view by asserting that if one "assumes" rather than merely "accepts" one's situation, then one transcends it. The nicety of this distinction—a crucial one in her ethics because the former term implies choice, the latter, submission —may escape many women. However, it permits Beauvoir to assert, quite correctly, that she has never opposed maternity and homemaking as long as they are "assumed," although she declares that "at the present time it is almost impossible to assume maternity in complete freedom."[18]

Beauvoir states at the end of the first chapter that biological factors are one of the keys to understanding women. However, since she is interested primarily in the social and cultural factors that help or hinder a woman's search for freedom and not in the biological factors that inevitably constitute part of the context within which that search must take place, she in effect tends to play down biological differences between the sexes.

Much of the criticism directed at *Le Deuxième Sexe* focuses precisely on Beauvoir's de facto minimization of the biological and psychological factors that constitute a woman's heritage. (Beauvoir is suspicious of psychoanalysis because it denies the idea of choice and, in its search for causes, is deterministic.) Indeed, author Suzanne Lilar devoted an entire book, *Le Malentendu du deuxième sexe* (The Misunderstanding of the Second Sex), to a refutation of *Le Deuxième Sexe*, accusing Beauvoir of, among other things, not taking into account the differences between male and female sex chromosomes. Lilar's shrill criticism falls short of its mark, for Beauvoir's point is simply that a woman's biological makeup does not condemn her to an existence of inane passivity nor to a life of repetitive, mindless drudgery.

Declaring that biological differences between the sexes do not explain woman's situation as the Other, Beauvoir rejects as inadequate and erroneous Freud's tendency to see in complex human situations nothing but sexual factors. She then examines Engels' history of woman as outlined in *The Origin of the Family, Private Property, and the State.* Engels affirms that before the discovery of metals there existed between the sexes a division of labor which, however, in no way implied inequality between them. With the discovery of bronze and with the appearance of the plow, man began to clear woodland and to cultivate ever larger and larger fields, an activity for which woman, because of her inferior physical strength, was unsuited. Man soon had recourse to the labor of other men whom he reduced to slavery. Private property appeared, and man, master of slaves and of the earth, became also the proprietor of woman.

Beauvoir agrees with Engels that the turning point of all history is the passage from the regime of community ownership to that of private property and that "woman was dethroned by the advent of private property."[19] Her lot, Beauvoir agrees, has for centuries been bound up with private property. But Engels does not explain how this passage came about. Indeed, he declares that "at present we know nothing about it." Nor does he suggest why the institution of private property necessarily resulted in the enslavement of women.

To answer these questions Beauvoir resorts to her basic postulates, which she fleshes out with other existentialist notions. "The original condition of the existent,"[20] she declares, is the inclination of the subject to think of himself as basically individual and to assert the autonomy and separateness of his existence. Before the invention of adequate tools, this basic impulse remained subjective and could not be carried out objectively. However, with the discovery of bronze and the subsequent fabrication of tools, man began to dominate nature; he began to see himself as an autonomous active force; he discovered himself as creator. Through challenge, struggle, and single combat each conscious individual strove to raise himself to sovereignty.

But, Beauvoir rightly says, the affirmation of the subject's individuality does not explain his attachment to property. Only by taking into account another feature of the existent's original condition can we understand the role that property plays for human beings. This feature is the tendency of each subject toward alienation—a tendency Beauvoir calls "an existential fact." Beauvoir explains that an awareness of human liberty creates a sense of anxiety in the subject and leads him to search for himself in things. This search is a kind of flight from self.

In the existentialist perspective, then, the existent succeeds in finding himself only in estrangement, in alienation. He discovers himself by identifying with something that is outside himself, which then becomes an image of himself. Alienation can be experienced authentically, in which case it is indistinguishable from the projects by which the existent continually transcends himself and his past. Or it can be experienced less authentically, as for example, in the case of a man whose property becomes an incarnation of the man himself. Indeed, a man can lose himself in his goods, which become as precious to him as his very life. Woman's muscular weakness, which prevented her from participating in man's physical domination of nature and thus from discovering herself as an autonomous, willful, and creative force, brought about her ruin because man regarded her simply in the perspective of his own project for enrichment and expansion.

However, Beauvoir says, we have still not ex-

plained why woman was oppressed or why the division
of labor between the sexes did not result in a friendly
association. She finds the explanation in the fact that
the human consciousness is imperialistic and seeks
always to expand its sovereignty in objective fashion.
"If the human consciousness had not included the
original category of the Other and an original aspiration to dominate the Other, the invention of the
bronze tool could not have caused the oppression of
woman."[21] Thus Beauvoir rejects the "economic mon-
ism of Engels" as she had rejected Freud's reduction
of the relationships between men and women to
sexuality.

Beauvoir does not, of course, reject Freud's or
Engels' theories *in toto*. On the contrary, she lauds
the Freudian insistence on the importance of the
body, for what an existent experiences as a body confronted with other bodies expresses his existential
situation concretely. Similarly, she accepts wholeheartedly the Marxist thesis that the ontological aspirations—the projects for becoming—of the existent
take concrete form according to the material possibilities offered. Neither Freudianism nor Marxism,
however, adequately explains woman's condition. Only
the existentialist notions concerning alienation and
the imperialism of the human consciousness explain
the historical fact of woman's enslavement and her
reduction to the status of either an object or an image.

Declaring that human society is not a natural
phenomenon but "an historical reality," Beauvoir
studies in the two long center sections of Volume One
the history of woman first as an object and second as
an image. Like nearly all the sections of *Le Deuxième
Sexe,* each of these units is constructed rather along
the lines of an academic demonstration. The opening
pages are devoted to an enunciation of the theme,

usually articulated in authoritative affirmations and assertions that follow each other in such rapid succession that the reader is bludgeoned into accepting them as the truth of the matter. Then follows a long series of examples drawn from books of the most diverse kind, usually arranged in roughly chronological order, and stitched together by commentary. This in turn is followed by a conclusion that summarizes the points made by the examples. The section ends with a reaffirmation of the principles and hypotheses stated in the opening pages.

Beauvoir's analysis of the various images that men have imposed on women and that women have been conditioned to accept as true images of themselves is entitled Myths. The study of the myths created around women was in fact Beauvoir's point of departure in writing *Le Deuxième Sexe*. Furthermore, this section was published in *Les Temps modernes* before the book appeared. Beauvoir asserts once again that in order to exist, man must renounce being and project himself toward a future yet unformed. But he also dreams of repose and plenitude. To satisfy this urge, he has made of the Other, of woman, an embodiment of peace, passivity, and delight—in short, an incarnation of his own dreams. However, since the conceiving consciousness necessarily views itself as the good, the Other is also an incarnation of evil. With elaborate argumentation Beauvoir weaves this double image of woman's otherness through dozens of pages.

Since women are made, not born, Beauvoir devotes the last section of Volume One to a study of the making of a woman and entitles it appropriately Formation. She analyzes the various elements that go into fashioning a woman's life from infancy through childhood, concluding with a study of sexual initiation. As a kind of postlude, she rounds out the volume with a chapter devoted to lesbianism.

Beauvoir's basic argument in this section is that for a boy there is no distinction between his vocation as a human being and his vocation as a male. "Humanity is male,"[22] she asserts in another of those aphorisms which reveal her fondness for the trenchant, incisive utterance that overstates and distorts the argument and that has provoked the ire of a number of readers. For a girl, however, there is a profound divorce between her condition as a human being and her vocation as a female. If adolescence is so difficult for girls, Beauvoir argues, it is because they must abandon the childhood image they have had of themselves as autonomous beings, as individuals, and accept the role of dependence and relative submission that society demands of them. They must pass from being essential to being unessential.

To sustain her argument, Beauvoir quotes from novels by women authors, from autobiographies of women, and from psychological studies. In particular, she cites numerous case histories from Wilhelm Stekel's study of abnormal psychology, *Frigidity in Woman in Relation to her Love Life*. One might wonder whether the fictional and autobiographical works of a few women writers who often made their sexual or emotional dilemmas the subject of their work (Isadora Duncan and Sophie Tolstoy are quoted at great length) and case histories taken from books on abnormal psychology constitute the best material from which to draw general conclusions concerning the formation of women.

In Volume Two of her study Beauvoir continues to quote extensively from the same works in order to illustrate her comments concerning the various roles society has traditionally expected a woman to fill: wife, mother, society matron, courtesan, dowager, etc. Central to Beauvoir's analyses, which advance slowly, borne down by the ever increasing weight of data, illustrative material, and extensive commentary, is that women, by the formation society has given them, are for the most part unable to engage in the kind of violent contact with the world that, for Beauvoir, gives life its flavor. "A woman," she says, "keeps busy, but she doesn't *do* anything. She is not recognized as an individual through her functions as a wife, mother, housekeeper. The reality of man is in the houses he builds, the forests he clears, the sick people he cures. But a woman, unable to fulfill herself through projects and goals, is forced to find her reality in the immanence of her person."[23]

Prevented from *doing* anything, women turn to various subterfuges in an attempt—occasionally ridiculous, often pathetic—to give content to their lives. They become narcissistic; or they identify completely with a man and thus participate vicariously in his independence at the expense of abdicating their own identity; or they turn to mysticism. Beauvoir studies each of these attitudes in chapters grouped together under the heading of Justifications. In her richly suggestive analyses of female narcissism, love, and mysticism, Beauvoir vigorously emphasizes that each of these attitudes is a kind of sterile hell in which a woman remains essentially trapped in her own subjectivity. Unable to affirm her freedom by constructive acts that leave a mark on society, she lives only marginally.

The final section of *Le Deuxième Sexe* is entitled "Vers la libération" (Toward Liberation). Economic emancipation, which can usually be achieved only if birth control is practiced, is the essential means by which women will be freed from dependence on men. Supporting her arguments with statistics, she writes pertinently about working conditions, education, birth control, and abortion. The ultimate liberation of

women will not be the result of a feminist struggle
against men. In fact, Beauvoir explicitly condemns
acerbic, polemical American feminists who conceive
of men as the enemy. The total liberation of women
will come about with the establishment of an authentically democratic society as announced by Marx.

In the final pages of *Le Deuxième Sexe* Beauvoir
reiterates a message that had been an underlying theme
of most of the works she wrote during the war years
—the theme of fraternity so closely allied in her
thought to the Resistance Movement and then later
to the general notion of resistance or revolt. She urges
men and women to join hands "as comrades, friends,
and partners"[24] in a common struggle to "abolish the
enslavement of half of humanity."[25] She concludes her
study with the words: "It is within the world given
to us that we must establish the reign of freedom. In
order to gain this supreme victory, it is necessary, for
one thing, that men and women rise above their
natural differentiation and unequivocally affirm their
brotherhood."

It is easy enough to criticize *Le Deuxième Sexe*
for this or that supposed flaw. Beauvoir no doubt fails
to come to grips with maternity and family life. She
no doubt advocates a kind of "virile independence"[26]
that is better suited to a woman who is unmarried,
childless, exceptionally intelligent, violently ambitious,
and relatively well-off (in short, like Beauvoir) than
to the majority of women.

Furthermore, the existentialist suppositions on
which the study rests are debatable. Beauvoir herself
wrote in 1963 that if she had to rewrite the book she
would give far greater importance to economic matters and far less to philosophical speculation about
the nature of consciousness. More specifically, she says
that she would base the notion of the Other, together

with the Manicheism it entails, not on an idealistic, *a priori* struggle pitting each consciousness against every other consciousness, but on the economic reality of supply and demand.[27] Although Beauvoir does not explain why she would build her study on a somewhat different foundation if she had it to do over again, any faithful reader of Sartre knows why. The reason is simply that in 1960 Sartre published *Critique de la raison dialectique* (Critique of Dialectical Reason), a mammoth philosophical and political treatise in which he argues that all human history has been a history of scarcity and a bitter struggle against shortage. In brief, Beauvoir would rewrite *Le Deuxième Sexe* to bring it in line with Sartre's revised philosophical and political theories. The most faithful of disciples, she clearly (and admittedly) takes her cue from Sartre in all matters relating to existentialist doctrine.

It is perfectly true that *Le Deuxième Sexe* suffers from a certain repetitiveness. Rather like a prosecuting attorney who brings in every scrap of evidence, Beauvoir builds up her case deliberately and without haste. Her strategy, not altogether unlike Montaigne's in his famous *Apologie de Raymond Sebond* (*Apology for Raymond Sebond*), is to accumulate evidence, to heap up data until the reader is overwhelmed ("discouraged" and "petrified" are Suzanne Lilar's words) by the mass of information. Only rarely does Beauvoir display her superb talent for satire; the pages in which she discusses certain male writers who have spoken arrogantly of women, notably Claude Mauriac and Montherlant, are written with marvelous verve and gusto. On the whole, however, the tone is earnest, humorless, and a bit pedantic.

Despite all the criticisms that have been leveled at *Le Deuxième Sexe*, the fact remains that it is the most important, the most forceful vindication of women's rights to have appeared in the twentieth century. In this book more than in any of her others, Beauvoir has realized her wish to leave a mark on the world. Not that she deluded herself into thinking that she could transform the condition of women. No significant change can come about, she insists, without the overthrow of capitalism. But she adds with excessive modesty, for her book has probably provoked more changes in individual lives than she can know of, that at least she has helped her female contemporaries to become conscious of themselves and of their situation.

In her autobiography Beauvoir notes that in 1949 she had for some time been thinking about writing a new novel. Not yet ready to talk about herself directly, she wished nevertheless to put herself into a book that would reflect her "feelings about life, death, time, literature, love, friendship, traveling." But she also wished to "portray other people and especially to relate the feverish and disappointing story of the years immediately following the war."[28]

Published in 1954 under the title of *Les Mandarins* (*The Mandarins*), Beauvoir's thousand-page novel is a vast fresco that depicts the rapturous joy with which a small group of Leftist intellectuals greeted the liberation of Paris in 1944 and the gradual shattering of their ardent hopes as they tried in vain, from 1944 to 1950 or thereabouts, to remake society according to their vision of a better world. Like Flaubert's *Education sentimentale* (*Sentimental Education*), *Les Mandarins* is the story of a failure of sorts.

As the war drew to a close, Beauvoir and her friends looked back on the war years as a period marked by solidarity, fraternity, and collective endeavor, a period during which their hopes for the future were intense, surely, but simple and unequivocal, for they awaited essentially one event—the Allied victory, "the triumph of Good over Evil."[29] After the war, Sartre and Beauvoir still refused to join the Communist party (they never would belong to the party) because they intended to speak out on issues as they saw them, supporting positions that were often close to those of the party but always reserving for themselves the right to deviate from party orthodoxy. With boundless energy Sartre, in particular, strove to organize the non-Communist Left into a viable political entity.

Beauvoir was far less interested in the practical aspects of politics—in meetings, strategy sessions, and public debates—although she was passionately interested in everything that provoked change. In 1948, while Beauvoir was working on *Le Deuxième Sexe*, Sartre and two friends attempted to found a political party, the R.D.R. (Rassemblement Démocratique et Révolutionnaire). Sartre's hope was that existentialism would eventually replace Marxism as the philosophy of the working class. However, French workers remained supremely indifferent to the R.D.R. Friends and sympathizers of the new party engaged in internecine struggles and bitter ideological quarrels, and Sartre's grandiose plans failed to materialize, leaving a certain feeling of bitterness and defeat, more it would seem in Beauvoir than in Sartre, who was soon engrossed in a host of other activities.

Friendships that had flourished at the end of the Occupation had, Beauvoir laments, been extinguished by 1949. *Les Mandarins*, she says, took shape around the death agony of friendships and of shared hopes. "Along with many other people, I had fallen from a heaven shared with friends into the dust of the earth.

The ground was strewn with broken illusions."[30] The underlying theme of the novel is precisely this descent from enthusiasm, intoxicating triumph, and rapture into the murky, unheroic business of daily existence, characterized by *taedium vitae,* by broken dreams, and by the specter of boredom.

This theme was a favorite of the romantics and again illustrates how broadly and pervasively Beauvoir's work, like that of many important twentieth-century writers, is colored by romanticism. Her despair, usually expressed as fear of old age and death, the histrionic aspect of this despair as well as the equally theatrical nature of her joy and exultation, her reforming zeal and desire to act, her insatiable thrust for experience, her earnest but also self-indulgent sincerity, her didacticism, her desire to be modern and to seize the real, her refusal to separate literature or art from life, her often repeated view that man strives for the impossible, for being, and falls back into the relative, into existence—all these are part of the enormously rich, romantic heritage that has determined so many of our attitudes in the twentieth century and that has sustained much of our literature and art.

Distinctly romantic, too, in its coloration is Beauvoir's dread of boredom, of a life that is quotidian, to use an expression made famous by Jules Laforgue, one of the gentlest and most timid of nineteenth-century French poets. Beauvoir's autobiography reveals a tendency on her part to dramatize the adventures and misadventures of her life so as to weave around herself a web of extraordinary events. Life during the Occupation was indeed exceptional. *Les Mandarins* traces the return to normalcy, to a life that is continually menaced by the humdrum and by boredom. Anne, one of the principal characters in the

novel and frequently Beauvoir's mouthpiece, speaks
of boredom in words very similar to those Beauvoir
used in her autobiography. "Boredom," muses Anne,
"is a scourge that has terrorized me ever since my
childhood. I wanted to grow up mainly to be able to
escape it, and I constructed my whole life around the
refusal of boredom."[31] This sentiment runs deep and
strong through the romantic temperament.[32]

In order to evoke the density, complexity, and
opaqueness of reality, Beauvoir uses in *Les Mandarins*
a technique she had used earlier. She alternates third-
person narrative chapters in which the central figure
tends to be Henri Perron, a former Resistance fighter,
author, and journalist, with chapters narrated in the
first person by Anne Dubreuilh, thirty-nine-year-old
wife of Robert Dubreuilh, a prodigiously famous
sixty-year-old author and founder of a leftist, non-
Communist political party. Events are thus seen from
different perspectives. Character is revealed, not
through authorial explanations, but through the
highly subjective appraisals that the various protagonists make of a situation.

Beauvoir's explanation of why she chose two
figures—one man and one woman—as her principal
subjects is interesting and gives small comfort to
those women liberationists who see in Beauvoir nothing but an apologist for feminism. A considerable
number of the things she wished to express in *Les
Mandarins* depended, she later noted, on the fact that
she was a woman, and so she chose to speak through
Anne. But she also wished to comment extensively on
the situation of a writer and on the political situation
of France in the years immediately following World
War II, and chose to express these views through a
man. Beauvoir answers the criticism that in her fictional world female characters never equal the male

characters in independence, that her women are never granted the active, energetic life led by her men, with the statement that her novels reveal what is, not what might be. Despite the fact that Anne is a distinguished psychiatrist (a career she seems to pursue only marginally and rather unconvincingly), her life is centered on her husband, her daughter, and later her lover.

Whereas Perron, Dubreuilh, and indeed most of the male characters throughout Beauvoir's fiction represent a point of view associated with "action, the finite and life,"[33] Anne incarnates, as do so many of Beauvoir's female characters, the opposite impulse— that toward being, toward an absolute, and toward death. "In Anne," Beauvoir comments, "I saw the negative aspect of objects whose positive side was revealed through Henri."[34]

Beauvoir's tendency to endow her female characters with "a sense of death and a taste for the absolute"[35] throws a curious light on one of the dubious assertions made in *Le Deuxième Sexe*. Here Beauvoir maintains that men often simultaneously cherish and fear women because they see in them an image of their own animal destiny, that is to say, death. Judging from her portrayal of Anne, it would seem that Beauvoir is projecting onto the male conscience a notion that is very much a part of her own attitude toward women.

When Beauvoir declares that Perron, because of his "joy in being alive, his eagerness to do things, his pleasure in writing,"[36] resembled her (Beauvoir) as much, perhaps even more than Anne, she is separating herself from the females she created in fiction and is situating herself clearly in the male world of joy and effort. She seems to accept with perfect ease the characterization of her that Sartre gave to an interviewer for Vogue in July, 1964: She possesses, Sartre said, a woman's sensibilities and a man's intelligence. Such a combination, Beauvoir suggests in her discussion of *Les Mandarins*, is exceptional. A person possessing this unique combination of qualities cannot serve as a model for the protagonist of a novel that is designed to reflect a more representative reality. Anne serves to incarnate Beauvoir's feminine sensibilities; but to incarnate her intelligence and creative energy Beauvoir felt she needed a man, and so created Perron.

The novel opens as Perron is on his way to a party celebrating the first peacetime Christmas in several years. He climbs the stairs and enters the apartment where the *fête* is taking place. It is probably significant that this party, "a real *fête*" as it is called, takes place in an upstairs apartment, for Beauvoir clearly associates the notion of *fête* with that of rising above the routine of everyday existence. This Christmas party marks the end of the war, but it also marks the celebration of the wartime way of life which, for the principal characters in the novel at least, was marked by clear-cut choices and dangerous, engrossing action. On the last page of the novel, Anne descends a flight of stairs and joins her family and friends in the garden. Beauvoir herself has pointed out that this descent represents Anne's return to the conventions and compromises of everyday life; it signals a kind of defeat that is inevitable, that is part of the very process of living.

Most of the novel's principal characters are assembled at the opening *fête*. Each will meet the peace differently as the wartime sentiment of fraternity melts away under the pressures of postwar realities. For Perron, tired of war and eager to be happy, the liberation of Paris is seen as a personal liberation. A pleasure trip to Portugal soon reveals to him the reality of human misery behind the façade of bright city lights. Editor of a Leftist newspaper, *L'Espoir* (Hope), he hopes to remain unattached to any political party. On the other hand, his friend and mentor, the Olympian Robert Dubreuilh, believes that a writer must engage actively in politics. Dubreuilh has recently founded a liberal-revolutionary party and urges Perron to commit *L'Espoir* to the new political organization. At first Perron refuses. As the clear-cut choices of wartime give way to the ambiguous and doubtful choices of postwar France, Perron is gradually drawn into situations in which the simple morality of right and wrong is no longer operative. When he, a former Resistance hero, perjures himself in court in order to save a girl with whom he is infatuated from being exposed as the former mistress of a Nazi captain, the whole problem of choice and responsibility becomes the Gordian knot it usually is in life itself.

The impossibility of making wholly acceptable choices is illustrated repeatedly in the long conversations between Perron and Dubreuilh. Using the novelist's privilege of telescoping historical events, Beauvoir moved certain events of the early fifties back to the years immediately following the war. Thus when the intellectual Left learns of the existence of Soviet slave labor camps it is torn between the desire to reveal the truth to the public, a disclosure which would play into the hands of the Right, and its belief that the U.S.S.R., despite its flaws, is still the world's best hope for a just society and the only bulwark against hated American imperialism.

Beauvoir's loathing of America's part in the Korean War, which was going on while she was writing the novel, helps explain her attitude toward American foreign policy. In the milieu in which *Les Mandarins* is set, it was axiomatic that the Soviet Union was preferable to the United States. Still, there runs through the novel a lucid and profound disenchantment with Russia as well as with America. In the case of Dubreuilh, the theme of disappointment in the course of political events gently melts into the theme of approaching old age.

Despite the restless activity of most of the characters and the often hectic pace of their lives—the all-night drinking bouts and the endless hours of work—they nearly all experience a sense of displacement, a curious nostalgia for a situation that they could be completely for or completely against. Beneath the furious rhythm of their lives there persists an elegaic strain that becomes more and more pronounced as the novel progresses. During the war, the major protagonists of the novel were all Resistance fighters, engaged in activities that were applauded by their society. During the postwar years, they saw themselves, as members of the left-wing intelligensia, eased from the center of political life. Political power eluded them, and they found themselves on the edge of society, performing the no doubt valuable function of witnesses, but no longer directly influencing the course of political events.

Beauvoir's original title of the novel, *Les Survivants* (The Survivors), suggests the mood in which the book was conceived. Later she intended to entitle it *Les Suspects*, a clearly ironic title pointing to the ambivalent situation of writers in society, especially left-wing existentialist writers like herself and Sartre. Since her chosen title had already been used by another author, a friend, Claude Lanzmann, suggested *Les Mandarins*, an equally ironic title. By equating herself and the intellectuals who were her friends with mandarins, Beauvoir clearly indicated the end of any illusions which existentialist authors might have had about joining the proletariat in a glorious march toward the future. In fact, *Les Mandarins* marks the end of the creative period of existentialism both as a philosophy and as a literary manifestation.

A host of younger writers and journalists cluster around Perron and Dubreuilh. That their lives and views are only occasionally illuminated helps to account for the novel's atmosphere of ambiguity and complex human relationships. Existence, Beauvoir had declared in *Pour une morale de l'ambiguïté,* is ambiguous, by which she meant that it has no one meaning. No existentialist novel better illustrates this notion than does *Les Mandarins.* Urgently, the characters discuss from multiple points of view the social, political, and intellectual problems of the day, making of *Les Mandarins* a rich and intricate chronicle of the concerns that preoccupied the French leftist intelligensia during the half dozen or so years following the war.

Interwoven into the texture of the novel are several love stories. The longest is Anne's affair with an American novelist, Lewis Brogan. Invited to a congress of psychiatrists in New York, Anne visits Chicago where she meets Brogan, who is, of course, modeled after Nelson Algren. (The names Brogan and Algren are quite similar in sound. Furthermore, *Les Mandarins* is dedicated to Algren.) The love affair between the two is a literary transposition (or imaginative distortion) of Beauvoir's relationship with Algren. The external events of the fictionalized account follow quite closely the account Beauvoir gives in her autobiography: the several trips to Chicago, the visits to bars and strip joints, the boat ride down the Mississippi and the quick visit to Central America, the stay in a cottage on Lake Michigan are all related in the novel.

Despite the obvious care with which Beauvoir

composed these episodes, the transatlantic love affair between Anne and Brogan remains curiously unreal. (Speaking to an interviewer in 1964, Algren suggests that by publicizing their affair in *Les Mandarins* Beauvoir showed that "the relationship could never have meant a great deal in the first place."[37]) It does, however, permit her to elaborate on a number of ideas concerning love and the feminine condition. Chief among them is that for a woman, the absence of love is the equivalent of death. None of Beauvoir's men would say as does Anne after the termination of her affair with Brogan: "My heart is no longer beating for anyone. It's as if it were no longer beating at all."[38]

Several critics have taken the position that Anne's love story is peripheral to what they believe to be the main focus of the novel, i.e., the chronicle of a certain segment of French society after the war, and thus should have been omitted. Beauvoir conceived the novel as a fictional transposition of her own life and to omit an episode as important to her as her relationship with Algren would have been unthinkable. Furthermore, the novel's basic themes, which are worked out in ethical and intellectual terms through the male characters, are worked out in emotional terms in Anne's story. To have omitted Anne's experiences in the United States would have been to deprive the novel of an emotional resonance that complements and extends the moral dilemmas of virtually all the characters. The theme of responsibility, which echoes throughout the entire novel, underlies Anne's relationship with her husband, her daughter, her friends, her patients. Dread of old age, a theme skillfully woven into the lives of several of the characters, is a powerful force in Anne's love for Brogan. It explains the note of quiet desperation that runs through Anne's account of their affair. After she and Brogan have separated once and for all, the reality of old age, which had been blocked out by her love, becomes so painfully visible that she contemplates suicide. Near the end of the novel Perron muses that "he used to believe that happiness was a way of possessing the world, while actually it was more like a way of protecting oneself against it."[39] Anne's affair with Brogan illustrates this important theme as surely as do Perron's and Dubreuilh's stories.

Paule, Perron's mistress of some ten years, belongs to that line of Beauvoir's heroines who abdicate their own individuality and try to live completely within their love for a man. She is a perfect example of the type of woman Beauvoir described disapprovingly in *Le Deuxième Sexe* in the chapter entitled "L'amoureuse" (The Woman in Love). "I love Henri with complete abnegation,"[40] she says. The problem is that Perron no longer loves her, a fact which Paule refuses to recognize. "Fundamentally, we are one single being,"[41] she deludes herself into thinking. Frantically she tries to resurrect the prewar days when Perron did in fact love her. In his unwillingness to hurt her, Perron becomes entrapped in a morass of half-truths and petty deceit as inauthentic as Paule's self-deception. Here again there is a delicately plotted concordance between the public and the private lives of the characters, between ethics and intimate emotional states.

On the verge of insanity, Paule undergoes psychiatric treatment. The only way her doctor can cure her is to bring her to the point of denying a love which had been the sole meaning of her existence for ten years. Once cured, she becomes a fat, banal woman. She has been cut off from her past. The past, however, is the very substance of one's being. In a revealing and somewhat startling statement that helps explain Beauvoir's penchant for fixing and redefining her own past, the author of *Les Mandarins* once told an interviewer: "If I do not adapt very well to change, perhaps it's because it frightens me. I like to build my own being, to *project* myself forward, but I must start from something *stable*."[42] Having no past to assume and to transcend, Paule has no real grasp on the present or the future. Totally uncommitted to any inner vision, she seems to have become singularly lifeless.

Nadine Dubreuilh is Anne's eighteen-year-old daughter. Brought up during the war years, she had loved a young Jew who was deported and died in a concentration camp. Her revolt against the world and her equally strong desire to live intensely have turned her into a rather neurotic young lady who seems unable to be nice to anybody and who, to assuage her injured spirit, hops into bed with countless men, especially American officers, with the perky remark that there is no better way for strangers to break the ice.

Toward the end of the novel Nadine, too, settles down to a more conventional life; she marries Perron and has a baby. The closing pages of the novel depict a domestic scene that contrasts sharply with the turbulence of the opening *fête*. The presence of a young couple with a baby (an extremely rare phenomenon in Beauvoir's fictional world) underscores the notion of a return to something approaching normalcy. The mandarins are quietly assembled in the garden mulling over possible titles for a new weekly magazine they intend to found.

In much of world literature, a garden—with its various (and sometimes contradictory) connotations of fertility, fecundity, enclosure, passivity, and repose

yet cultivation—is richly symbolic. Usually it evokes
female images suggesting life. To depict a rejection of
the ethics of heroism and a return to a less heady but
more normal condition of life, Beauvoir uses the traditional but nonetheless effective image of a garden.
Furthermore, the notion of life is emphasized by the
presence of a baby and by a discussion concerning the
birth of a new journal. The intellectuals of the Left
who played a crucial role in the Resistance, or at least
who thought they did, have become more or less rec-
onciled to their status as revered and honored authors,
but ineffectual political leaders.

Les Mandarins has a breadth of historical perspective, a density, and a richness of texture that make
it wholly worthy of the Prix Goncourt it won in 1954.
Writing in the early sixties, Beauvoir declared that
most of the fiction published during the fifties, especially the *nouveau roman*, completely ignored the
momentous events that shaped postwar Europe. "So
many things," she said, "have happened since 1945,
and fiction has scarcely expressed any of them. Future
generations that might want to learn about us will
have to consult works on sociology, statistics, or simply
read our newspapers."[43] They would also have to read
Les Mandarins, but not just because it is a fine chronicle. Beauvoir insists that an imaginative projection of
experience, as distinguished from a mere chronicle of
events, conveys the "significance" of experience. That
is precisely what *Les Mandarins* does. It recaptures
the human significance of ethical and political problems that were intensely personal and emotional concerns for Beauvoir, Sartre, and their friends among
the non-Communist Left during the years immediately
following the war.

Beauvoir's seriousness of purpose in *Les Mandarins* is wholly admirable. If the novel falls short

of being great, it is once again because Beauvoir lacks
the imaginative intensity that characterizes supreme
creators of fiction. Her vision is simply not powerful
enough to enable her to formulate in fictional characters the schemes of redemption and enlightment
that effect an expansion of the reader's own moral
vision or awareness.

Furthermore, the novel provides the reader with
few pleasures of style. Indeed, the prose is by and
large colorless and graceless, marked by colloquialisms
and occasional vulgarity. It will not do to say, as
several critics have, that the author of *Les Mandarins*
simply does not write well. Beauvoir's shift toward
a style that strikes many readers as leaden and undis-
tinguished is probably one consequence of her postwar loss of faith in literature as something sacred.

French critic Serge Julienne-Caffié has suggested
that the dialogue in *Les Mandarins* is the linguistic
equivalent of the socialist and democratic state which
the characters in the novel (they all speak quite similarly) wish to see established in France. It is certainly
true that in *Les Mandarins* and in most of her subsequent books Beauvoir contemptuously rejects any
belletristic attitude toward literature, an attitude she
proclaims to be eminently bourgeois.

There may be yet another explanation for Beauvoir's inclination to write prose that often seems
deliberately pedestrian, consciously limited to the
spoken language. Despite their vitality and their incessant activity, Beauvoir's mandarins are ultimately
shown as living not in the world of action but in what
Nietzsche called "the prison house of language." Momentous social and political forces are at work shaping
the world around them while they, infatuated with
their own words, talk on and on, only dimly aware
of the fact that no one is really listening. Indeed, in

Beauvoir's work subsequent to *Les Mandarins* there runs, beneath the ever-fierce capacity for outrage in the face of certain kinds of injustice and the ever-keen curiosity about the contemporary world, an acute awareness of the limitations of literature and even of language in a world in which two-thirds of the human population suffers from hunger, in which torture of political enemies is not uncommon, and in which racism and economic exploitation are as prevalent as ever.

Still, beneath the surface texture of language that is at times perversely charmless, a reader of *Les Mandarins* can discern—particularly in the pages that are dominated by the female characters—the peculiar current of emotionalism, tenderness, and lyricism, intense yet discreet, that runs stealthily through all of Beauvoir's works and that combines with the author's intellectual toughness to create a literary voice unmistakably her own. Flawed though it may be, *Les Mandarins* must surely be counted among the most significant French novels published since World War II.

5

Ending

in Earnest

Beauvoir has written only one extended piece of literary criticism—an eighty-page essay on Sade. In 1951, an editor at Gallimard invited her to contribute a study on an author of her choice to a proposed collection of essays on famous writers. She chose Sade.

In June of that same year, Beauvoir completed the first draft of *Les Mandarins* and, putting it aside until Sartre could read it during the summer holidays, she plunged into her essay on Sade, which first appeared in *Les Temps modernes* under the title of "Faut-il brûler Sade?" ("Must We Burn Sade?"). In 1955, shortly after the considerable commercial success of *Les Mandarins*, Gallimard collected three of Beauvoir's longer essays—the one on Sade, "La Pensée de droite, aujourd'hui" (What the Right Is Thinking Today), and "Merleau-Ponty et le pseudo-Sartrisme" (Merleau-Ponty and Pseudo-Sartrism)—and published them in book form under the title of *Privilèges* (Privileges).

"Faut-il brûler Sade?" harks back to Beauvoir's moral phase. Her interest in Sade, whom she did not know well before working on her essay, may well have been aroused by Sartre's somber assertion toward the end of *L'Être et le néant* that there are only two possible lines of conduct open to us in our relationship with other people: we may try to make ourselves the sort of object in the eyes of the Other that we would wish to be, or we may try to take away the Other's freedom. The first, Sartre says, finds its extreme expression in masochism, the second in sadism. Indeed, Beauvoir is primarily interested in using Sade's life and works as an illustration of the existentialist notion of the Other. She saw in Sade's personality a dramatic confrontation between man as transcendence and man as object.

Beauvoir's study of Sade was obviously influenced

by Sartre's striking but controversial study of Baudelaire (1947). In *Baudelaire*, Sartre had used the kind of psychoanalytic approach to literary criticism that he would use again in his inordinately long *Saint Genet* and still later in his monstrously huge study on Flaubert, which runs into thousands of pages.

Admitting that we know very little about Sade's childhood, Beauvoir portrays the twenty-year-old marquis as being essentially in accord with his society. It is true that he probably engaged in sexual excesses, but such behavior was tolerated among members of the aristocratic class to which he belonged. In fact, Beauvoir interprets such behavior as an attempt on the part of young provincial aristocrats, who had little concrete power, to act out in brothels their illusions of sovereignty. Sade was little different from his peers, she suggests.

Then, in the autumn of 1763 a scandal broke out. Several girls who worked in a brothel which Sade frequented brought charges against their client, accusing him of indulging in sexual perversions. On the King's orders, Sade was arrested and imprisoned in Vincennes Fortress, where he spent a fortnight before being released. Beauvoir maintains that as a result of his imprisonment, Sade, at the age of twenty-three, made a decisive choice. Because society called his pleasures criminal, he decided that henceforth he would *be* a criminal. From 1763 on, eroticism became for him a form of revolt against society.

Since the essence of existentialist ethics is freedom of choice, Beauvoir argues that Sade's deliberate decision to become a dedicated criminal and to seek pleasure in crime was an eminently ethical act, authentic and wholly worthy of admiration. Sartre had maintained that the seven-year-old Baudelaire, after his mother's remarriage, deceived himself into believing

that he was "forever alone." Henceforth he repudiated
all social obligations and deliberately cultivated a
form of dandyism which was, in effect, bourgeois
and reactionary. Sartre condemns Baudelaire soundly
for choosing to be what he believed himself destined
to be, whereas Beauvoir praises Sade for doing precisely the same thing. From the standpoint of existentialist ethics there is very little difference between
the two cases. The reason for Sartre's condemnation
of Baudelaire and Beauvoir's approval of Sade is
simply that Baudelaire eventually sided with political conservatives whereas Sade became an enemy
of the bourgeoisie. In short, although both Beauvoir
and Sartre seem to claim that choice has its own moral
validity, it is clear that they can only approve of
choices which conform to the doctrines of the political
Left or which are determined by the mystic of revolution. (Thus Sartre praises the twentieth-century author, Jean Genet, for choosing to be a criminal after
he heard himself called a thief.) Ethics has in fact
given way to politics.

Beauvoir's post-1950 tendency to subordinate
ethical to political concerns was clearly evident in
Les Mandarins. It would continue to mark much of
her later work. In fact, one of the most distressing
features of the third volume of the autobiography is
Beauvoir's inclination to view as an enemy anyone
who does not share her political convictions. Such an
attitude is hardly the perfect stance for a writer who
presents long portions of her autobiography—especially the section dealing with the decade of the fifties
—as a faithful chronicle of events. Beauvoir seldom
if ever declares that her dislike, often hatred, for this
or that person is simply the result of opposing political views. Instead, she nearly always denigrates individuals who disagree with her by cataloging their

supposed moral flaws, their alleged weaknesses of character.

Beauvoir's malevolence toward her erstwhile friend Camus, who broke with Sartre over the question of rapprochement with the Communists, is singularly unpleasant. Fortunately, Camus was famous enough to have his defenders. However, as critic François Bondy has pointed out, it is saddening to think that Beauvoir's distorted attacks on less famous people, many of whom were dead when the autobiography appeared, remain unchallenged. Her attack on the great Russian writer Boris Pasternak, whose opposition to tyranny, even Soviet tyranny, irked Beauvoir, is straightforward enough. However, her complacent approval of the decision by Soviet authorities to send Olga Ivinskaya, Pasternak's companion, to a slave labor camp after the writer's death, is distressing.

The increasing stridency of Beauvoir's voice in the second half of *La Force des choses*, the hardening of her political views, the implacability of her enmity, must be seen as intensely personal reactions to the political situation in France during the fifties, in particular to the role of the French army in Indochina and Algeria. Beauvoir's horror of torture, which the French army routinely practiced in Algeria as a means of keeping the North African state a French colony and of suppressing the indigenous movement for political independence, her rage against the terrorism in which the French army engaged under the guise of maintaining law and order, are deeply felt and run, like a somber leitmotif, through her account of the fifties.

Beauvoir's despair was increased by the hypocrisy of the French government's official position (publicly decrying torture while privately permitting it) and by the public's desire not to know the unpleasant truth. "I am an intellectual," she wrote. "I place great value on words and on the truth. Every day, all day long, I was bombarded with lies that were being spat out of every mouth."[1] At times, her loathing for France became so intense that she would spend days in her apartment rather than go out into the street and mingle with Frenchmen who were indifferent to the suffering inflicted on thousands of Algerians in the name of French grandeur. "I hated everything," she notes, "this country, myself, the world. And I told myself that when all is said and done the most beautiful things—although I had loved and been deeply affected by them—are really not so beautiful. They could have blown up the Acropolis and Rome and all the earth, and I would not have raised a finger to stop it."[2]

Obviously Beauvoir expresses her despair in language that is grandly oratorical and histrionic. Like the romantics to whom she is close in so many ways, she refuses to separate literature from life. Her concern and her anger are admirable, indeed vastly preferable to the apathy and egotistical resignation of those who close their eyes to injustice and complacently accept the established order of things.

When the case of Djamila Boupacha, a young Algerian girl who had been tortured by French soldiers, finally reached the courts (after elaborate attempts by military and governmental officials to quash the affair), Beauvoir did everything in her power to expose the facts to the French public. She served as president of a citizens' Committee for Djamila Boupacha and, with the collaboration of Gisèle Halimi, the defense attorney in the case, prepared a documentary account of the proceedings which was published in 1962 under the title of *Djamila Boupacha*. (The

public remained largely indifferent and, despite the
general consensus that the French military and civilian
authorities in Algeria were guilty of serious crimes,
they were not indicted.)

It is with an awareness of Beauvoir's mood in the
fifties that one must read *La Longue Marche*, 1957
(*The Long March*), her account of the visit she and
Sartre made to China in the autumn of 1955. In many
respects Beauvoir has the temperament of a believer.
"I have a taste for the permanent and the absolute,"[3]
she once wrote—an assertion that places her squarely
on the side of Calvin, Pascal, and Rousseau (whose
Confessions she rediscovered with joy late in life) and
that separates her from Montaigne, Voltaire, and
Camus. Her hope that the Western nations would turn
to socialism after World War II had proved to be
illusory. Any faith she may have had in the capacity
of the French government to curb the excesses of the
French army in Algeria had vanished by the mid-
fifties. Her confidence in the U.S.S.R. had been temp-
ered somewhat by the revelation of the existence of
Soviet labor camps and would soon be put to a severe
test when Soviet tanks crushed the abortive revolution in Hungary in 1956 (Beauvoir condemned the
Soviet Union for its repression of the Hungarian up-
rising). There remained, however, China—that enormous and mysterious country which, for a time at
least, was the focus of her hopes for a better world.

La Longue Marche, which is in part an answer
to the strongly unfavorable reports on Communist
China which the French journalist Robert Guillain
had published in 1956, is, by Beauvoir's own admis-
sion, the most outdated of her books. Although Beauvoir occasionally recounts her own experiences, the
book is mainly a compilation of historical, economic,
and sociological information on China, grouped in

chapters that bear titles such as Peasants, The Family, Industry, Culture.

Beauvoir's title refers not only to the famous thousand-mile march across China by Mao Tse-Tung and his band of followers, but also to her vision of Communist China as a country "which is in a state of perpetual change," a land in which "the present derives its meaning from the past which it transcends and from the future which it ushers in."[4]

Beauvoir clearly imposes on China a grid of vocabulary and reference which derives from existentialism. Ever since World War II, she has made much of comradeship which, for her, can only be realized by striving for a common political goal. She has had a *dream* of fraternal endeavor, although she has but seldom had the experience. China seemed to incarnate her dream. Here, the project of each individual (a notion central to Beauvoir's ethics) was identical with and inseparable from the collective enterprise.

Eager to praise China's accomplishments under Mao's leadership, Beauvoir peppered her book with statistical data which, she realized at the time, would soon cease to be valid. The pedantic tone of the book and the heavy emphasis on statistics make for very turgid reading. Despite occasional vignettes that have a flicker of life, *La Longue Marche* is the most leaden of Beauvoir's books.

"The most important, the most irreparable thing that has happened to me since 1944," noted Beauvoir in the early 1960s, "is that I have grown old."[5] Indeed, the theme of old age and the closely related theme of death had always been present in Beauvoir's work, but they had remained in the background, much like a menacing cloud on the horizon. During the 1950s, when Beauvoir was in her forties, her disenchantment with the political scene in Europe was exacerbated (or perhaps partly provoked) by her realization that she was growing old. The ten or so books she wrote from 1950 to 1972 are all, with the exception of *La Longue Marche*, marked by a deepening awareness of old age.

Beauvoir's distress at the thought of growing old was at first attenuated by a new love affair. In 1952 she was forty-four years old. Claude Lanzmann, a talented writer seventeen years her junior, was an ardent Marxist and a contributor to *Les Temps modernes*. The two of them spent several days together in Holland and in December, 1952. After their return to Paris, they decided to live together. This arrangement in no way affected Beauvoir's relationship with Sartre, which since her twentieth year has been the stabilizing element in her life. Because she was unwilling to give up her two-month summer holiday with Sartre, and since the prospect of not seeing Lanzmann for two months was painful to her, all three parties agreed that sometime in the middle of the holidays Lanzmann would join the other two for ten days or so. The attempt to work out a *ménage à trois* in the 1930s had been unsuccessful, largely, it seems, because of Beauvoir's jealousy of Olga. This time it was much more successful. Sartre, it would appear, was not at all jealous.

Lanzmann's spontaneity and sheer exuberance infused into Beauvoir a new sense of vitality and joy. "Sartre, most of my friends, myself—we were all puritans," she remarks. "We were careful about our reactions. We seldom externalized our feelings."[6] Lanzmann's presence freed her temporarily from her age, and in 1953, while working on the final version of *Les Mandarins*, she was happy, enclosed within the joy of her private life.

During the next several years Beauvoir not only continued to write at her usual steady pace, but also to travel a good deal, usually with Sartre, sometimes with Lanzmann, occasionally with the two of them. Always eager to see new sights and to extend her contact with the world, Beauvoir made trips to the Soviet Union, China, Africa, Brazil, Cuba, and later, Japan. She traveled extensively in Europe, often by car for she had bought an automobile in 1951 and enjoyed driving. Beginning in 1955 she and Sartre decided to spend their summers in Rome, Beauvoir's favorite city.

In 1958 Beauvoir and Lanzmann separated. The initiative, she says, came from him. Although she had never expected their liaison to last indefinitely, still she found the separation painful. "The last tie that held me back and prevented me from recognizing my true state suddenly broke,"[7] she comments. At the age of fifty, she saw herself standing on the threshold of old age. Friends with whom she had shared her younger years began to die: Richard Wright, who had introduced her to New York, Merleau-Ponty. . . :

I sat watching, helplessly, the play of external forces: history, time, death. In the face of the inevitable, I no longer had even the consolation of tears. Regrets, fits of rebelliousness—I had exhausted them all. I was vanquished; I gave up. Hostile to the society to which I belonged, banished by age from the future, little by little stripped of the past, I was reduced to my own naked presence. How icy cold![8]

After wishing for several years to write about herself directly, Beauvoir began working on her autobiography in the autumn of 1956. "Growing old," she once remarked, "is a process of defining and delimiting oneself."[9] Seen in this light, the writing of an autobiography—a work in which she defines herself and reduces herself to a "naked presence"—is part of Beauvoir's awareness of growing old.

But for her, writing was also a way of keeping old

age at bay. "A writer has the good fortune of being able to escape petrifaction during the time he is actually writing. Each page, each sentence requires fresh inventiveness, a decision for which there is no precedent. Creation is adventure; it is youth and freedom."[10]

Beauvoir distinguishes sharply between the nature of fiction and that of autobiography. She believes that a novel, however loosely constructed, ends up conveying a sense of an inevitable sequence of events. It cannot convey the sense of uncertainty, of limitless possibilities, of an unformed future which is characteristic of experience. On the other hand, she believes that in an autobiography she can present events in all their gratuitousness, their apparent meaninglessness, and thus remain closer to experience. "There is a danger," she recognizes, "that through this capricious profusion, the reader, unable to distinguish any clear image, will see only a jumble."[11]

No reader would accuse the first volume of the autobiography, *Mémoires d'une jeune fille rangée* (1958), of being "a jumble." It is one of Beauvoir's most rigorously composed books. She herself explains that if this volume has more unity than the others it is because her childhood and adolescence were guided by a clear and overriding goal: to become an adult. The last three volumes—*La Force de l'âge* (1960), *La Force des choses* (1963), and especially *Tout compte fait* (1972)—are in fact marked by the presence of gratuitous and seemingly meaningless details (lists of films she has seen, books she has read, records she has listened to) that annoy some readers but that, for others, convey to a remarkable degree the sense of contingency, the untidiness of life itself.

In the autumn of 1963, shortly after the publication of *La Force des choses*, Beauvoir, who was in

Rome, received a call from Paris informing her that her seventy-seven-year-old mother had fallen and broken her leg. Friends had transported the elderly lady to a hospital.

Beauvoir returned to Paris immediately. Upon further examination it was discovered that Mme de Beauvoir was suffering from cancer. Because she had always been afraid of dying from cancer, she was not told the truth. Rather, she was led to believe that she had peritonitus. Her case was soon judged hopeless. She declined rapidly and, about a month after her fall, she died. When Beauvoir's sister commented to one of the nurses about her mother's dreadful suffering during the final two weeks, the nurse replied: "I assure you, Madame, that it was a very easy death."[12]

Beauvoir, along with her sister, had spent hours at her mother's bedside during the dying woman's final illness. A few days later after the funeral, Beauvoir felt compelled to write an account of her mother's death, and spent the winter of 1963-64 working on it.

Une Mort très douce, 1964 (*A Very Easy Death*), which Beauvoir called a *récit*, is one of her shortest books. Sartre has called it her best. On one level, it is an almost clinical, at times harrowingly dispassionate, account of an old woman dying of cancer in a modern hospital. The contrast between the messiness of life (the tears, the cries of pain, the pus, the unpleasant body odors, the soiled sheets, the vomiting) and the cool efficiency of modern medical technology (the various machines attached to her mother's body, the doctors themselves, well groomed, well paid, and condescending) is all the more striking because it is understated. Beauvoir's language can be as sharp, as clean, as impersonal as a scalpel. With remarkable skill, she paces her account of her mother's decline in such a way that when death comes the reader experiences, as in a good tragedy, relief from the intolerable anguish that has steadily mounted.

The anguish, however, is essentially Beauvoir's own and not her mother's. On another level, then, *Une Mort très douce* is an epilogue to *La Force des choses*. It is part of Beauvoir's autobiography.

Watching her mother die, Beauvoir feels compassion for the old woman's ravished and anguished body. She cannot forget, however, that her mother is a member of the hated French bourgeoisie. "I was saddened," Beauvoir writes, "by the contrast between the reality of her suffering body and the nonsense with which her head was stuffed."[13] Beauvoir's portrait of her dying mother is thus composed of two contrasting tones: compassion for the suffering body and ironic contempt for the old woman herself, for the life she led, and for the values she professed.

When Mme de Beauvoir remarked that she was glad to be in Hospital C. because she had heard that it was so much better than Hospital G., Beauvoir, by the very way she tells the incident, turns the trivial comment into yet another example of the fatuous vanity of the bourgeoisie. Since Mme de Beauvoir was not told that she was dying of cancer, Beauvoir weaves the theme of deceit into her account of her mother's death. Cunningly she equates the atmosphere of hypocrisy which surrounds the dying woman with the atmosphere of falsehood that characterized (in Beauvoir's view at least) the bourgeois milieu in which her mother had lived. The two kinds of falsehoods (if indeed they are falsehoods) are of a totally different order. By deliberately blurring the distinction between them, Beauvoir indulges in a kind of sophistry that mars not a few pages of her work.

In the middle of the book, Beauvoir devotes an

entire chapter to an account of her mother's childhood and youth. She portrays her mother as having
a character in many ways similar to her own. Molded
by the values of the bourgeois milieu in which she
was reared, her mother was unable to free herself
from the prejudices of her society. "She lived," Beauvoir assures us, "at odds with herself."[14] Although
Beauvoir as a child had adored her mother, during
adolescence she came to see in Mme de Beauvoir a
symbol of everything she herself despised. Beauvoir's
choices in life—choices which she liked to think were
free—were in fact often dictated by her wish to do
the opposite of what her mother would have ap-
proved.

Beauvoir's inability to see her mother except
through ideological lenses is chilling. Although elsewhere she has written eloquently about the difficulty
of communicating with others and about the opaqueness of the Other, she seems to believe that her mother
was perfectly transparent, so shallow (or bourgeois)
was she. The cavalier way in which she passes judgment on her mother borders on arrogance. There is
scarcely a page in *Une Mort très douce* that is not
informed by the author's ironic glance.

Usually Beauvoir's sister spent the night in their
mother's hospital room. One night when Beauvoir
instead of her sister arrived for the night, Mme de
Beauvoir looked at her elder daughter and murmured:
"You frighten me."[15] One can well understand the
old woman's reaction.

"Why was I so deeply moved by my mother's
death?"[16] asks Beauvoir in the last chapter. The answer is implicit in the whole book. She saw in her
mother's death an intimation of her own. In her
mother's suffering body she saw her own aging body.
Beauvoir's attitude toward her mother's death is illu-

minated by words she was to publish some six years later in her study of old age. "The death of someone who is close to us, of a friend," Beauvoir wrote in *La Vieillesse*, "deprives us not only of a presence but also of that whole part of our life which was entwined with theirs. People older than we carry away with them our own past when they die."[17] The grief in *Une Mort très douce* is genuine, but it is not grief at her mother's death. In the final analysis, the book is an elegy in which Beauvoir laments the dissolution of her own being.

For eight years (1956-64) Beauvoir had been pre-occupied with the composition of the first three volumes of her autobiography. After the publication of *Une Mort très douce* she wished to return to fiction and for about a year worked on a novel dealing with old age. After returning from her summer holiday in October, 1965, she reread the first draft and found it so bad that she abandoned the work entirely. The theme, however, was to crop up in one form or another in each of her next four books.

Turning to another project, Beauvoir wrote a short novel which was published in 1966 under the title of *Les Belles Images* (the same title in the English edition). In the fourth volume of her autobiography, Beauvoir explains that her intent in *Les Belles Images* was not essentially to describe in detail the experience of any one of the various characters but to capture the tone and inflexion of the language of chic Parisians living in the consumer-oriented French society of the 1960s. Beauvoir insists that she tried to maintain as great a distance between herself and this "technological society"[18] as possible, although she felt that she was continually bombarded with its slogans and clichés through radio, newspapers, magazines, and advertising. To prepare for the actual writing of the novel, she sifted through books and journals, studiously collecting the inane, pretentious, and silly expressions that seemed to her to characterize the speech mannerisms of the wealthy French bourgeoisie.

The obvious danger in writing a novel composed largely of platitudinous dialogue is that the reader, instead of shuddering at the emptiness and vacuity of the bourgeois way of life—which he is clearly meant to do—might well find the book dull and unrewarding. Smart tittle-tattle about stereo sets, vacations in Bermuda, and ultra-modern architecture palls very quickly.

The principal character, Laurence, is married to an up-and-coming architect, has two daughters, and works for an advertising agency where she has been very successful designing advertisements for things like tomato sauce. The title of the novel is an ironic reference to the "lovely images" she creates.

Each of the characters in the novel is minutely intent on keeping up appearances and on projecting an acceptable image of himself—an image as slick, as artfully deceptive as those created by Laurence. Unlike the other characters, who seem to have no reality beneath the glib image they project, Laurence senses dimly that her life is somehow out of joint. As the result of three incidents, her vague malaise becomes a full-scale existential crisis which is accompanied by nausea (a rather worn image, coming nearly thirty years after Sartre's *La Nausée*).

The first incident involves Laurence's ten-year-old daughter, who has just become aware of the fact that misery and suffering exist in the world. "Mama," the child asks, "why do we exist?"[19] In attempting to answer her daughter's question, Laurence is more or less forced to recognize, at least temporarily, the reality of unhappiness and suffering. Uneasy thoughts

of starving millions, of Vietnam, and of secret guilt
flit through the novel.

The second incident occurs one night as Laurence
is driving back to Paris from a weekend stay in the
country. She is behind the wheel. Her husband is
sitting beside her. Suddenly a cyclist swerves in front
of the car. To avoid hitting him, Laurence runs the
car into the ditch. No one is hurt, but the car is
demolished. Later her husband tells her that the
cyclist was clearly at fault and that if she had hit him
several witnesses would have testified in her favor.
Suddenly, it dawns on her that her husband thinks
she should have hit the cyclist, saving them the expense of a new car. For a moment (but only for a
moment) she is repelled by his crassness.

Lastly, she witnesses the suffering of her mother,
Dominique, a woman in her fifties who had clawed
her way to the top of the business world. For several
years Dominique has been living with Gilbert, one of
the richest men in Paris. She had imagined that they
would grow old (and even richer) together. Now,
however, Gilbert announces that he plans to abandon
her and marry a nineteen-year-old girl, the daughter
of one of her rivals. Dominique is such a thoroughly
disagreeable person that a reader may be excused if
he feels a twinge of uncharitable pleasure at the
thought that she finally gets her come-uppance. Laurence, however, shares her mother's suffering. Grief,
anguish, rage are not "lovely images." They are the
raw stuff of authentic experience as contrasted to the
artificiality of carefully contrived images.

Eventually Dominique returns to her ex-husband,
Laurence's father. Considerable confusion has existed
among readers over Beauvoir's attitude toward the
aging man. Throughout most of the novel he lives
alone, praises the joys of solitude, of good books, good
food, good music. Since he seems not to share the

thirst for success and the passion for wealth that
distinguishes the other characters, some readers have
believed that he expressed Beauvoir's own ideas and
values. Nothing could be further from the truth, and
Beauvoir has clarified this point in the last volume
of her autobiography. He represents the traditional
values of the bourgeoisie as surely as the others represent the new bourgeois values. He is as egotistical,
as indifferent to social ills, especially to the suffering
of millions of people, as any of the other characters
in the novel. His reunion with Dominique is Beauvoir's affirmation that the traditional, "cultured"
bourgeoisie and the new managerial class, the techno-
crats, are one and the same class.

Laurence's disillusionment never reaches the intensity of a crisis of consciousness. Largely unarticu-
lated, it is expressed through her body, for she becomes ill and cannot eat. Her malaise certainly does
not assume the form of a rejection of the social class
to which she belongs. However, in the final pages of
the novel, Laurence, nauseated by her awareness of
the fact that the lovely images around her conceal the
emptiness of her life (again the theme of boredom),
tries to save her daughter Catherine from being in-
doctrinated with the sterile bourgeois values that have
made her own life insufferably vapid. Earlier, at the
urging of her husband, she had reluctantly agreed to
send her daughter to a psychiatrist who, hopefully,
would make the child less sensitive to the suffering
and unhappiness of others. (As usual in her postwar
works, Beauvoir tends to see suffering only in terms of
the injustices which the privileged bourgeoisie of the
West inflicts on less privileged social classes.) Hoping
that her daughter might have a more authentic life
than she has had, Laurence now refuses to subject
Catherine to further psychiatric treatment:

"No," she shouted. Not Catherine. I'll not let them do to her what they did to me. What did they do to me? They made me into this woman who loves no one, who is insensitive to the beauties of the world, incapable even of weeping—this woman whom I'd like to vomit out. Catherine. With her I'll do just the opposite; I'll let her see the truth immediately, and perhaps a ray of light will filter down to her, perhaps she will be able to escape. Escape what? Night. Ignorance, indifference.[20]

Les Belles Images contains many of Beauvoir's usual themes. However, they are here expressed in images that are facile, pat, and rather too obvious. Eager to jolt the reader into contempt for the bourgeoisie, Beauvoir has indulged her taste for didacticism at the expense of imaginative insight.

Scarcely had Beauvoir finished *Les Belles Images* when she began another fictional work, *La Femme rompue*, 1968 (*The Woman Destroyed*), a collection of three novellas. Each has an aging woman as protagonist. Each is a variation of one of the most persistent themes in Beauvoir's work: women's dependence on men for a sense of their identity. In *Le Deuxième Sexe* Beauvoir had analyzed the peculiar difficulties women experience in liberating themselves from the Other. In each of the three novellas that comprise *La Femme rompue*, she shows a woman who has put all her eggs in one basket, namely, marriage. In each case it turns out to have been an unwise thing to do. However, the fault lies not essentially in marriage nor in the husbands who, tired of their aging spouses, have turned elsewhere for companionship and solace. It lies with the women themselves for having failed to fashion a personal identity independent of their husbands and children, and for being utterly incapable of accepting the devastating truth

that they are no longer necessary to anyone. Unable
to face reality squarely, they weave around themselves
a web of delusions that prevents them from communicating with other people. Alone and lonely, they
face the future with terror. Only in the first story,
"L'Âge de discrétion ("The Age of Discretion") does
the heroine finally succeed in re-establishing a dialogue of sorts with her husband.

The very form of the other two stories suggests
the inability of the protagonists to break down the
walls of deception that they have erected between
themselves and other people. The second story is a
long rambling monologue reminiscent of Molly Bloom's
famous monologue at the end of Joyce's *Ulysses*. The
speaker is a lower-class woman who devotes a New
Year's Eve to a bitter, spiteful recollection of her life.
Unwilling to accept responsibility for her failures, she
distorts reality so as to make everyone else responsible. Clearly Beauvoir intends that behind the speaker's
monologue of sophisms, self-deceptions, sick imagin-
ings, and hate we discern the figure of an odious
woman.

The third story, which is the title story, is written
in the form of a diary, and chronicles the six-month
ordeal of Monique, a middle-aged woman who discovers that her husband is infatuated with a young,
ambitious, and aggressive woman lawyer. Instead of
facing up to the situation (exactly what Beauvoir
thinks her heroine should do is not made clear),
Monique sinks into a morass of speculation and self-
deception. By refusing to recognize the fact that her
husband no longer loves her, she turns away from
the truth and cuts herself off from reality—the only
thoroughly reprehensible act in Beauvoir's scheme of
things.

Each of the three female voices that emerge from

La Femme rompue tells a tale of disintegration, pro-
digious bad faith, and, above all, overweening egotism. They are the hysterical voices of women who
are too monstrously selfish, too lacking in perception
to be entirely credible as fictional characters. Furthermore, Beauvoir's vulgar and pedestrian prose—a prose
that ultimately strikes the reader as an unpleasant
affectation—is leaden and oppressive, adding to the
generally sodden effect of the book. In the final analysis, both *Les Belles Images* and *La Femme rompue*,
skillfully constructed as they may be, are decidedly
inferior to Beauvoir's best fictional work.

For several years Beauvoir had been haunted by
the theme of old age—a theme which, in fact, had
been woven into the fabric of her last four books.
Now she decided to treat the subject directly and to
write a socio-anthropological study on old age that
would be comparable in scope and importance to her
famous study on women.

Her interest in the subject was two-fold. At the
end of *La Force des choses* she had touched on the
problems of aging. Hostile critics had responded with
sententious pronouncements about the serenity and
wisdom of old age. Beauvoir wished to denounce the
myths and blatant lies that society has perpetrated
about the aging, for it is these lies that enable society
to ignore in good conscience the deplorable psychological, physical, and economic state of the vast majority of the world's old people. Like *Le Deuxième
Sexe, La Vieillesse,* 1970 (*The Coming of Age*), is an
indictment of society and an exposure of a truth that
has been conveniently ignored. It is a denunciation
of the conspiracy of silence that has surrounded the
suffering of the aged. Here Beauvoir, the former
schoolteacher, is in her natural element, rubbing our

noses in an unpleasant truth which we have stubbornly refused to see.

She had an even more fundamental reason for studying old age. "I feel the need to perceive the broad implications of whatever condition is my own," she notes. "As a woman, I managed to explain the feminine condition. As I approached old age, I wished to understand what it means to be old."[21] Indeed, the axis of all of Beauvoir's works is clearly the author herself.

La Vieillesse is divided into two parts. Using basically the same approach she had used in *Le Deuxième Sexe*, Beauvoir first examines the biological implications of old age and the various attitudes toward old people from antiquity to the present. Always a diligent researcher, she scanned literary, historical, and sociological works in her search for the innumerable references to aging and the aged that make up the body of her book. As in *Le Deuxième Sexe*, the strategy is to accumulate such a mass of information that the reader is bludgeoned into accepting the author's viewpoint. While this kind of romp through the centuries and through civilizations as diverse as those of Western Europe, China, and primitive Oceanian tribes invariably provides the reader with information, it also lays the author open to the charge of superficiality. Few specialists in any one of the numerous areas and academic disciplines Beauvoir touches upon are likely to be satisfied with her comments. Still, the ponderous mass of material she has assembled is impressive.

The second part of *La Vieillesse* is entitled "L'Être-dans-le-monde" (Being-in-the-world). Relying heavily on statistics and on the diaries and accounts of old people, Beauvoir analyzes the situation of the elderly from various perspectives. Basically she shows that society relegates the old person to the role of the

Other. Refusing to explain the often lamentable situation of many old people by biological factors alone, Beauvoir emphasizes the economic distress that frequently makes old age such a terrifying ordeal. "The elderly," Beauvoir stresses, "submit to a biological destiny which necessarily has economic consequences: they become unproductive."[22] They are thus sacrificed to productivity.

But their drama is also an existentialist drama. They have no future and hence no project. They cannot transcend their past in an energetic élan toward the future. They remain inert. For them "the world falls silent."[23]

To the extent that it is biologically determined, the situation of the elderly would seem to be rather more insoluble than that of women. However, Beauvoir's condemnation of the callous contempt with which society too often treats its elderly is perfectly justified. Half measures, she asserts, will be unable to correct the situation. Only when society rejects the notion that an individual's worth can be measured in terms of his productive capacity will it be possible to alleviate some of the anxieties associated with old age. As far as the individual is concerned, "we should wish to keep throughout our old age those passions that are strong enough to prevent us from being preoccupied with ourselves. Life remains worthwhile as long as we attach value to the lives of other people— value determined by love, friendship, indignation, compassion." Beauvoir concludes that "we must live a life so committed, so justified, that we can continue to cherish it even when all our illusions are lost, and our ardor for life has cooled."[24]

After writing a book about old age, Beauvoir felt inclined to continue her autobiography and to recount her own old age. (Actually she recounts her life from 1963 to 1972, when she was in her late fifties and early sixties.) Published in 1972, the fourth volume of the autobiography is called *Tout compte fait (All Said and Done)*.

Instead of following a strictly chronological sequence, Beauvoir organized her material around certain broad themes. Thus, in the first chapter she looks back and relates in condensed form the most decisive events and encounters in her life. People whom she had known in the thirties and who figure in earlier volumes of the autobiography surprisingly reappear after an absence of many years. With marvelous verve Beauvoir describes the transformations they have undergone. Unhampered by the necessity of conveying an ideological message, she indulges her talent for creating characters. Indeed, many of the people who appear in her autobiography are far more memorable than the rather wooden figures who populate much of her fiction.

Succeeding sections of *Tout compte fait* are devoted to various subjects: dreams Beauvoir has had, literature, movies, theater, art, travel, and accounts of public events in which she participated. More discursive and ruminative than the previous volumes, *Tout compte fait* bears somewhat the same relationship to the complete autobiography that Montaigne's third and final book of essays bears to his entire *Essays*. Both authors seem ultimately to establish a curious kind of distance between the self and the world. Not that either loses interest in the surrounding world. On the contrary, in none of Montaigne's essays is the physical world with its clutter, its jumble of things and sensations more present than in the essays of the last book. And in none of Beauvoir's books is the everyday hum of life, the trivia of daily existence, more pervasively present than in *Tout compte fait*. From her leisurely enumerations of weekends spent in the country, museums visited, books read, films seen and music heard, there clearly emerges the unmistakable voice of the author who is intent on defining the meaning of her private experience.

It is a voice that is as steady as ever but somewhat more subdued, less abrasive—a voice tinged, certainly not with sadness or fatigue, but with a sense of inevitable conclusion. "I have a keen awareness of my finitude," Beauvoir says simply. "Even if my creative work will encompass two or three more volumes, it will remain what it is."[25]

Beauvoir's fear of death has subsided. Her anguish at the thought of dying had always been the reverse side of her intense desire to live and to be happy. The tendency of certain critics to present Beauvoir as a kind of brooding *Melancolia*, neurotically preoccupied with death, is a travesty. Obviously, death figures prominently among her concerns, as it does among those of most thinking people. But awareness of death is precisely a manifestation of life. "The idea of death," wrote Beauvoir in *La Vieillesse*, "provokes a reflex toward life."[26]

No longer fearing death, she has renounced rebelling against it. Like Montaigne, who ultimately cultivated an attitude of unconcern, even disinterest in the face of death, Beauvoir, albeit in a graver register, notes with surprise that she has become "semi-indifferent" toward her own eventual demise. "I no longer feel the anguish of death which was so violent in my youth," she observes. Still, the idea of her own death is never far from her mind; "I have the feel of nothingness in my bones."[27]

But she also continues to have in her bones a passion for writing. "Writing," she says, "has remained the principal business of my life."[28] Declaring that a writer does not convey a body of knowledge but communicates "the feeling of his being as actually

lived in the world,"[29] Beauvoir has striven in all her
works to describe the world as she has seen it and to
organize and structure her experience in such a way
that it can become part of the reader's experience.
"The writer," she affirms, "tries to establish commu-
nication with others from the standpoint of his own
unique experience."[30]

Still, Beauvoir insists that her work is not essentially documentary, and warns her readers—a warning
that few critics have heeded—that in her work "the
I who speaks remains separated from the *I* who lived,
just as each sentence remains separated from the experience that is at its origin." A writer who wishes
to communicate not just the facts but also the flavor
of his life "creates a work that does not translate
reality, but that exists in the realm of the imaginary.
Such a writer fashions a fictional self."[31]

On the last page of *Tout compte fait* Beauvoir,
with a remarkable sense of plenitude, notes that she
has written the very books she had hoped to write
when she was twelve years old. Having rejected the
notion of writing for posterity, she always wished to
write for her contemporaries. Looking back on her
many books, she concludes her autobiography with
remarks that are both a summing up and a succinct
statement of the distinctive nature of her literary
opus:

I have not been a virtuoso of writing. I have not, like
Virginia Woolf, Proust, or Joyce, resuscitated the shimmer
of sensations nor caught in words the external world. But
such was not my intention. I wished to make myself exist
for other people by communicating to them, in the most
direct way, the flavor of my own life. I have pretty well
succeeded. I have made adamant enemies, but I have also
made many friends among my readers. That is all I
wanted.[32]

NOTES

Translations of titles of Simone de Beauvoir's works that have been published in English are given in quotation marks or in italics. For works not translated into English, a literal translation of the title has been provided. All translations appearing in the text are my own.

1. The Dutiful Daughter

1. *Mémoires d'une jeune fille rangée.* "Collection Folio." (Paris: Gallimard, 1958), p. 265.
2. *La Force de l'âge.* "Le Livre de Poche." (Paris: Gallimard, 1960), p. 10.
3. *Pyrrhus et Cinéas* in *Pour une morale de l'ambiguïté suivi de Pyrrhus et Cinéas.* "Collection Idées." (Paris: Gallimard, 1944, p. 247.
4. *Mémoires d'une jeune fille rangée*, p. 11.
5. A.-M. Henry o.p., *Simone de Beauvoir ou l'échec d'une chrétienté* (Paris: Librairie Arthème Fayard, 1961), p. 102.
6. *Mémoires d'une jeune fille rangée*, p. 64.

7. Ibid., p. 83.
8. Ibid., p. 48.
9. Ibid., p. 57.
10. Ibid., p. 22.
11. Ibid., pp. 14-15.
12. Ibid., p. 58.
13. Ibid., p. 190.
14. Ibid., p. 192.
15. Ibid., p. 503.
16. *Tout compte fait* (Paris: Gallimard, 1972), p. 27.
17. *Mémoires d'une jeune fille rangée*, pp. 378-79.
18. Ibid., p. 201.
19. Ibid., p. 195.
20. Ibid., p. 196.
21. Ibid., p. 201.
22. Ibid., p. 251.
23. Ibid., p. 480.
24. Ibid., p. 482.

2. *Transcending the Past*

1. *La Force de l'âge.* "Le Livre de Poche." (Paris: Gallimard, 1960), p. 19.
2. Ibid., p. 541.
3. Ibid., p. 26.
4. Ibid., p. 23.
5. René Girard, "Memoirs of a Dutiful Existentialist," *Yale French Studies*, 27 (1961), 44.
6. *La Force de l'âge.* p. 102.
7. Ibid., p. 293.
8. Ibid., p. 293.
9. Ibid., p. 51.
10. Ibid., p. 239.
11. *Mémoires d'une jeune fille rangée*, p. 320.
12. *La Force de l'âge*, p. 106.
13. Ibid., p. 145.
14. Ibid., p. 630.

15. Girard, p. 44.
16. *La Force de l'âge*, p. 420.
17. Ibid., p. 699.
18. Ibid., p. 298.
19. Ibid., p. 299.
20. Ibid., p. 626.
21. *L'Invitée*. "Le Livre de Poche." (Paris: Gallimard, 1943), p. 8.
22. Ibid., p. 8.
23. Ibid., p. 9.
24. *Mémoires d'une jeune fille rangée*, p. 197.
25. *L'Invitée*, p. 28.
26. *La Force de l'âge*, p. 245.
27. Elaine Marks, *Simone de Beauvoir: Encounters with Death* (New Brunswick, N.J.: Rutgers University Press, 1973), p. 30.
28. *L'Invitée*, p. 28.
29. Maurice Cranston, "Simone de Beauvoir," in *The Novelist as Philosopher*, ed. John Cruickshank (London: Oxford University Press, 1962), p. 175.
30. *L'Amérique au jour le jour* (Paris: Editions Paul Morihien, 1948), p. 104.
31. *L'Invitée*, p. 158.
32. *Pyrrhus et Cinéas* in *Pour une morale de l'ambiguïté suivi de Pyrrhus et Cinéas*, p. 255.
33. *L'Invitée*, p. 131.
34. Ibid., p. 218.
35. Ibid., p. 187.
36. *L'Amérique au jour le jour*, p. 316.
37. *L'Invitée*, p. 300.
38. *La Force de l'âge*, p. 396.
39. *L'Invitée*, p. 380.
40. Ibid., p. 380.
41. Francis Jeanson, *Simone de Beauvoir ou l'entreprise de vivre (suivi de deux entretiens avec Simone de Beauvoir)* (Paris: Le Seuil, 1966), p. 276.
42. Ibid., p. 276.
43. *Pyrrhus et Cinéas*, p. 283.
44. *L'Invitée*, p. 511.
45. Ibid., p. 511.

46.   *La Force de l'âge*, p. 391.
47.   Ibid., p. 630.
48.   Ibid., p. 630.

3.   Ethics and the Moral Phase

1.   *Pyrrhus et Cinéas*, p. 233. Montaigne also relates this
      anecdote at the end of Essay 42, Book I: "De l'ine-
      qualité qui est entre nous" ("Of the inequality that is
      between us").
2.   *Pour une morale de l'ambiguïté*, p. 147.
3.   Goethe, *Faust*, Part I, ll. 3249-50:

          So tauml' ich von Begierde zu Genuss,
          Und im Genuss verschmacht ich nach Begierde.

4.   *Pyrrhus et Cinéas*, p. 363.
5.   Ibid., p. 300.
6.   Claude Lévi-Strauss, *Tristes Tropiques* (Paris: Plon,
      1956), p. 45.
7.   *La Force de l'âge*, p. 632.
8.   *Pyrrhus et Cinéas*, p. 327.
9.   *La Force de l'âge*, p. 633.
10. Like many of the major incidents in Beauvoir's nov-
      els, this one is based on an event in the author's life.
      In *Mémoires d'une jeune fille rangée* (p. 183), Beau-
      voir discusses the death of the infant son of the family
      maid, Louise, and says that this was her first encounter
      with grief. The incident is also related in *Pyrrhus et
      Cinéas* (p. 241).
11. *Le Sang des autres*, p. 37.
12. Ibid., p. 13.
13. Ibid., p. 21.
14. Ibid., p. 22.
15. Ibid., p. 23.
16. Ibid., p. 152.
17. *Tout compte fait* (Paris: Gallimard, 1972), p. 465.
18. François Bondy, "Notes on a Lady Mandarin," *En-
      counter*, 25 (October 1965), 89.
19. *Tout compte fait*, p. 33.

20. Ibid., p. 33.
21. Ibid., p. 33.
22. *Le Sang des autres*, p. 91.
23. Ibid., p. 25.
24. Ibid., p. 147.
25. *Mémoires d'une jeune fille rangée*, p. 98.
26. Ibid., p. 477.
27. *La Force de l'âge*, p. 31-32.
28. *Le Sang des autres*, p. 43-44.
29. Ibid., p. 44.
30. *La Force de l'âge*, p. 625.
31. *Le Sang des autres*, p. 300.
32. Ibid., p. 300.
33. Ibid., p. 300.
34. Ibid., p. 44.
35. Ibid., p. 38.
36. C. B. Radford, "Simone de Beauvoir: Feminism's Friend or Foe?" *Nottingham French Studies*, Part I: VI, No. 2 (October 1967), 87-102, and Part II: VII, No. 1 (May 1968), 39-53.
37. *Les Bouches inutiles* (Paris: Gallimard, 1945), p. 54.
38. Ibid., p. 81.
39. Ibid., p. 101.
40. Ibid., p. 79.
41. Ibid., p. 113.
42. Ibid., p. 41.
43. Ibid., p. 91.
44. The phrase is by one of Beauvoir's friends of the thirties, Raymond Aron, who used it for the title of one of his influential books.
45. *La Force des choses*, I. "Collection Folio." (Paris: Gallimard, 1963), p. 98.
46. *Tous les hommes sont mortels* (Paris: Gallimard, 1946), p. 49.
47. *Le Sang des autres*, p. 58.
48. *La Force des choses*, I, p. 234.
49. *Tous les hommes sont mortels*, p. 16.
50. Ibid., p. 14.
51. Ibid., p. 60.
52. *La Vieillesse* (Paris: Gallimard, 1970), pp. 196-97.

53. *Tout compte fait*, p. 50.
54. In Italian, *fosco* means somber, gloomy. Further, the names of Fosca and Faust are similar in sonority, for in French, Faust is pronounced with a closed o.
55. Beauvoir's fictional city, Carmona, bears a marked resemblance to the real Italian city, Cremona.
56. *Tous les hommes sont mortels*, p. 239.
57. Jean-Paul Sartre, *L'Être et le néant* (Paris: Gallimard, 1943), p. 168.
58. *Pyrrhus et Cinéas*, pp. 253-54.
59. Ibid., p. 252.
60. *Tous les hommes sont mortels*, p. 75.
61. Ibid., p. 108.
62. Ibid., p. 343.
63. *La Force des choses*, p. 15.
64. Novalis, *Fragmente* (Dresden: Wolfgang Jus, 1929), p. 219, Fragment 572.
65. *Pour une morale de l'ambiguïté*, p. 13.
66. Ibid., p. 184.
67. Ibid., p. 196.

4. No Time for Boredom

1. *Revelations* 3:16.
2. *La Longue Marche* (Paris: Gallimard, 1957), p. 308.
3. *L'Amérique au jour le jour* (Paris: Paul Morihien, 1948), p. 7.
4. Ibid., p. 328.
5. *La Force des choses*, I, p. 180.
6. Ibid., p. 177.
7. Ibid., p. 176.
8. Ibid., p. 176.
9. Ibid., p. 344.
10. Ibid., p. 376.
11. Ibid., p. 136.
12. Ibid., p. 258.
13. *Le Deuxième Sexe*, I. "Collection Idées." (Paris: Gallimard, 1949), p. 34.
14. Ibid., p. 17.

15. Ibid., p. 193.
16. Ibid., p. 285.
17. Ibid., p. 67.
18. *Le Deuxième Sexe*, II, p. 455.
19. *Le Deuxième Sexe*, I, p. 104.
20. Ibid., p. 71.
21. Ibid., p. 74.
22. Ibid., p. 15.
23. *Le Deuxième Sexe*, II, p. 353.
24. Ibid., p. 497.
25. Ibid., p. 504.
26. Ibid., p. 266.
27. *La Force des choses*, I, p. 267.
28. Ibid., p. 269.
29. Ibid., p. 360.
30. Ibid., p. 360.
31. *Les Mandarins*, I. "Collection Folio." (Paris: Gallimard, 1954), p. 299-300. In *Mémoires d'une jeune fille rangée*, Beauvoir writes (p. 94): "I couldn't bear boredom, which soon turned into anguish. I hated idleness."
32. The early nineteenth-century romantic, Benjamin Constant, wrote: "Fear of boredom is the dominant force in my life." Cited by Henri Peyre, *Qu'est-ce que le romantisme* (Paris: Presses Universitaires Français, 1971), p. 126.
33. *La Force des choses*, I, p. 369.
34. Ibid., p. 362.
35. Ibid., p. 363.
36. Ibid., p. 367.
37. H. E. F. Donohue, *Conversations with Nelson Algren* (New York: Hill and Wang), p. 269.
38. *Les Mandarins*, II, p. 498.
39. Ibid., p. 441.
40. Ibid., p. 195.
41. *Les Mandarins*, I, p. 295.
42. Francis Jeanson, *Simone de Beauvoir ou l'entreprise de vivre (suivi de deux entretiens avec Simone de Beauvoir)* (Paris: Le Seuil, 1966), p. 289.
43. *La Force des choses*, II, p. 458.

5. Ending in Earnest

1. *La Force de choses*, II, p. 120.
2. Ibid., p. 431.
3. Ibid., p. 93.
4. *La Longue Marche* (Paris: Gallimard, 1957), pp. 405-6.
5. *La Force des choses*, II, p. 501.
6. Ibid., p. 15-16.
7. Ibid., p. 237.
8. Ibid., p. 415.
9. Ibid., p. 503.
10. Ibid., p. 504.
11. Ibid., p. 296.
12. *Une Mort très douce* (Paris: Gallimard, 1964), p. 137.
13. Ibid., p. 28.
14. Ibid., p. 55.
15. Ibid., p. 102.
16. Ibid., p. 158.
17. *La Vieillesse* (Paris: Gallimard, 1970), p. 389.
18. *Tout compte fait* (Paris: Gallimard, 1972), p. 139.
19. *Les Belles Images* (Paris: Gallimard, 1966), p. 29.
20. Ibid., p. 254.
21. *Tout compte fait*, p. 148.
22. *La Vieillesse*, p. 95.
23. Ibid., p. 484.
24. Ibid., p. 567.
25. *Tout compte fait*, p. 44.
26. Ibid., p. 360.
27. Ibid., p. 50.
28. Ibid., p. 131.
29. *La Vieillesse*, p. 422.
30. *Tout compte fait*, p. 132.
31. *La Vieillesse*, p. 423.
32. *Tout compte fait*, p. 513.

Bibliography

I. Simone de Beauvoir's Works

L'Invitée. Paris: Gallimard, 1943. *(She Came to Stay*, tr. L. Drummond. London: Secker and Warburg, 1949; *She Came to Stay*, tr. not indicated. Cleveland and New York: World Publishing Company, 1954.)

Pyrrhus et Cinéas. Paris: Gallimard, 1944.

Le Sang des autres. Paris: Gallimard, 1945. *(The Blood of Others*, tr. Roger Senhouse and Yvonne Moyse. New York: Alfred A. Knopf, 1948.)

Les Bouches inutiles. Paris: Gallimard, 1945.

Tous les hommes sont mortels. Paris: Gallimard, 1946. *(All Men are Mortal*, tr. Leonard M. Friedman. Cleveland and New York: World Publishing Company, 1955.)

Pour une morale de l'ambiguïté. Paris: Gallimard, 1947. *(The Ethics of Ambiguity*, tr. Bernard Frechtman. New York: Philosophical Library, 1948.)

L'Amérique au jour le jour. Paris: Paul Morihien, 1948. *(America Day by Day*, tr. Patrick Dudley. New York: Grove Press, 1953.)

L'Existentialisme et la sagesse des nations, "Idéalisme moral et réalisme politique," "Littérature et métaphysique," "Oeil pour oeil." Paris: Nagel, 1948.

Le Deuxième Sexe, vol. I, "Les Faits et les mythes," vol. II, "L'Expérience vécue." Paris: Gallimard, 1949. *(The Second Sex,* tr. H. M. Parshley. New York: Alfred A. Knopf, 1953.)

Les Mandarins. Paris: Gallimard, 1954. *(The Mandarins,* tr. Leonard M. Friedman. Cleveland and New York: World Publishing Company, 1956.)

Privilèges, "Faut-il brûler Sade," "La Pensée de droite, aujourd'hui," "Merleau-Ponty et le pseudo-sartrisme." Paris: Gallimard, 1955. *(Must We Burn Sade?,* tr. Annette Michelson. London: Peter Nevill Ltd., 1953.)

La Longue Marche. Paris: Gallimard, 1957. *(The Long March,* tr. Austryn Wainhouse. Cleveland and New York: World Publishing Company, 1958.)

Mémoires d'une jeune fille rangée. Paris: Gallimard, 1958. *(Memoirs of a Dutiful Daughter,* tr. James Kirup. Cleveland and New York: World Publishing Company, 1959.)

Brigitte Bardot and the Lolita Syndrome. London: Deutsch, Weidenfeld and Nicholson, 1960.

La Force de l'âge. Paris: Gallimard, 1960. *(The Prime of Life,* tr. Peter Green. Cleveland and New York: World Publishing Company, 1962.)

Djamila Boupacha, in collaboration with Gisèle Halimi. Paris: Gallimard, 1962.

La Force des choses. Paris: Gallimard, 1963. *(Force of Circumstances,* tr. Richard Howard. New York: G. P. Putnam's Sons, 1964.)

Une Mort très douce. Paris: Gallimard, 1964. *(A Very Easy Death,* tr. Patrick O'Brian. New York: G. P. Putnam's Sons, 1966.)

Les Belles Images. Paris: Gallimard, 1966. *(Les Belles Images,* tr. Patrick O'Brian. New York: G. P. Putnam's Sons, 1968.)

La Femme rompue, "Monologue," "L'Age de discrétion." Paris: Gallimard, 1967. *(The Woman Destroyed,* tr. Patrick O'Brian. London: Collins, 1968.)

La Vieillesse. Paris: Gallimard, 1970. *(The Coming of Age,* tr. Patrick O'Brian. New York: G. P. Putnam's Sons, 1972.)

Tout compte fait. Paris: Gallimard, 1972. (*All Said and Done*, tr. André Deutsch. New York: G. P. Putnam's Sons, 1974.)

II. Works on Simone de Beauvoir

A quite extensive bibliography of newspaper and journal articles on Simone de Beauvoir can be found in *La Nature chez Simone de Beauvoir* by Claire Cayron, Paris: Gallimard. 1973.

Algren, Nelson. "The Question of Simone de Beauvoir," *Harpers'* (May, 1965), pp. 134-36.

Bays, Gwendolyn. "Simone de Beauvoir: Ethics and Art," *Yale French Studies*, I (1948), pp. 106-12.

Bondy, François. "Notes on a Lady Mandarin," *Encounter* (October, 1965), pp. 85-89.

Brombert, Victor. "Simone de Beauvoir and *Le Sang des autres*," in *The Intellectual Hero*. Philadelphia and New York: J. B. Lippincott Company, 1961, pp. 232-38.

Cayron, Claire. *La Nature chez Simone de Beauvoir*. Paris: Gallimard, 1973.

Cranston, Maurice. "Simone de Beauvoir," in *The Novelist as Philosopher*, ed. John Cruickshank. London: Oxford University Press, 1962, pp. 166-82.

Donohue, H. E. F. *Conversations with Nelson Algren*. New York: Hill and Wang, 1964, pp. 178-86, 266-69.

Fitch, Brian T. " 'Le Dévoilement de la conscience' de l'autre: *L'Invitée* de Simone de Beauvoir," in *Le Sentiment d'étrangeré chez Malraux, Sartre, Camus et S. de Beauvoir*. Paris: M. J. Minard, 1964, pp. 143-72.

Gagnebin, Laurent. *Simone de Beauvoir ou le refus de l'indifférence*. Paris: Éditions Fischbacher, 1968.

Gennari, Geneviève. *Simone de Beauvoir*. Paris: Éditions Universitaires, 1958.

Girard, René. "Memoirs of a Dutiful Existentialist," *Yale French Studies*, 27 (1961), pp. 41-46.

Henry, A.-M. *Simone de Beauvoir ou l'échec d'une chrétienté*. Paris: Librairie Arthème Fayard, 1961.

Hourdin, Georges. *Simone de Beauvoir et la liberté.* Paris: Les Éditions du Cerf, 1962.

Jaccard, Annie-Claire. *Beauvoir.* Zurich: Juris Verlag, 1968.

Jeanson, Francis. *Simone de Beauvoir ou l'entreprise de vivre (suivi de deux entretiens avec Simone de Beauvoir).* Paris: Le Seuil, 1966.

Julienne-Caffié, Serge. *Simone de Beauvoir.* Paris: Gallimard, 1966.

Lasocki, Anne-Marie. *Simone de Beauvoir ou l'entreprise d'écrire.* The Hague: Martinus Nijhoff, 1971.

Lilar, Suzanne. *Le Malentendu du Deuxième Sexe.* Paris: Presses Universitaires de France, 1969.

Marks, Elaine. *Simone de Beauvoir: Encounters with Death.* New Brunswick, N.J.: Rutgers University Press, 1973.

Merleau-Ponty, Maurice. "Le Roman et la métaphysique," in *Sens et non-sens.* Paris: Nagel, 1948, pp. 45-71.

Moubachir, Chantal. *Simone de Beauvoir ou le souci de différence.* Paris: Éditions Seghers, 1972.

Nahas, Hélène. *La Femme dans la littérature existentielle.* Paris: Presses Universitaires de France, 1957.

Peyre, Henri. *French Novelists of Today.* New York: Oxford University Press, 1967, pp. 292-307.

Radford, C. B. "The Authenticity of Simone de Beauvoir," *Nottingham French Studies,* IV, No. 2 (October, 1965), pp. 91-104.

―――. "Simone de Beauvoir: Feminism's Friend or Foe?" Part I, *Nottingham French Studies,* VI, No. 2 (October, 1967), pp. 87-102.

―――. "Simone de Beauvoir: Feminism's Friend or Foe?" Part II, *Nottingham French Studies,* VII, No. 1 (May, 1968), pp. 39-53.

Reck, Rima Drell. "Simone de Beauvoir: Sensibility and Responsibility," in *Literature and Responsibility.* Baton Rouge, La.: Louisiana State University Press, 1969, pp. 86-115.

Strichland, G. R. S. "Beauvoir's Autobiography," *The Cambridge Quarterly,* I (Winter 1965-66), pp. 43-60.

Van der Berghe, Christian Louis. *Dictionnaire des idées: Simone de Beauvoir.* The Hague: Mouton, 1967.

INDEX